BATHROOM BOOK

of

CAT TRIVIA

Humorous, Heartwarming, Weird & Amazing

Diana MacLeod

BLUE
BIKE
BOOKS

The Publisher: Blue Bike Books

Library and Archives Canada Cataloguing in Publication

MacLeod, Diana, 1956–
    Bathroom book of cat trivia / Diana Macleod.

Bathroom Book of Cat Trivia
ISBN-13: 978-897278-26-0
ISBN-10: 1-897278-26-8

    1. Cats—Miscellanea. I. Title.
SF445.5.M32 3007   636.8   C2007-901525-5

Project Director: Nicholle Carrière
Project Editor: Wendy Pirk
Production: Michael Cooke, Trina Koscielnuk
Illustrations: Peter Tyler

PC: P5

DEDICATION

To my husband Lloyd, daughters Tarra and Jodie and, of course, the felines living under my care that have treated me like their own.

CONTENTS

ACKNOWLEDGEMENTS

Well, here we are, the end of my journey and the beginning of yours. It has been an enlightening and engaging adventure delving into the corners of the feline world where I had never ventured. This labor of love would not have been possible if not for all the cat writers before me—their work proved invaluable.

Many hands touched what you are holding in yours, and I am grateful for the expertise and talent used to pull together all the elements that made it happen, especially the outstanding efforts of Wendy Pirk, my editor.

Animals have been a big part of my life, both personally and professionally. Life on this planet would be a very dismal affair without companion animals, not to mention the enjoyment I receive daily, and their unconditional acceptance of me as their shepherd.

INTRODUCTION

Dogs come when they're called; cats take a message and get back to you later.

–Mary Bly

Felines, more specifically domestic cats, are a species humans have yet to master. Just ask someone who has ever tried to put a collar and leash on a cat and take the critter for a walk. Still, with their growing popularity among humans, cats will eventually usurp mans' best friend the dog from the number one position as the family pet.

The fur-clad members of the family Felidae have a fascinating history dating back to before the ancient Egyptians, yet it is that culture that elevated the cat to god-like status.

And cats have not forgotten that.

Did you know that Cardinal Richelieu of France had 14 cats as roommates? His feline family was so important to him that they had their own servants. When he died in 1642, guess who inherited all his worldly goods? That's right, his beloved cats.

There is no shortage of names for cats, but one of the most commonly used names is Puss. During the Egyptian era of worshipping cats, it is thought that Puss evolved from the name of Egypt's powerful moon goddess, Pasht, with whom cats were associated, making them sacred and worthy of our praise.

This book is full of other amazing bits of history, headlines, antics and funky facts about cats that could fuel the game show *Jeopardy* and its host, Alex Trebeck, until retirement.

Pounce through the pages, grinning like a Cheshire cat.

CATS' CROSSING

Building the Purrfect Pet

Researchers delving into the origin of cats reveal the formula behind today's family pet—sex, time and travel. Over time, carnivorous felines migrated and mated to create the animal that would become the unique pet that humans love to fawn over.

Based on DNA samples taken from living species, geneticists traced the arrival of felines to North America, via a land bridge across the Bering Strait between the Siberian Peninsula and Alaska, back nine million years—two million years after the creatures appeared in Asia.

Feline migrations back and forth across the Bering Strait over the years as sea levels waxed and waned resulted in the evolution of diverse members of the cat family, including the most successful cat of all—*Felis silvestris.*

Cat Tree

Mating, time and travel resulted in eight branches of the cat family tree, known as Felidae. Not content to stay home, the four-legged opportunists made at least 10 intercontinental migrations, colonizing most of the world. Australia likely became inhabited with domesticated cats later than the other continents as a result of escapees from ships and later by the arrival of Europeans and their pets. With the exception of Antarctica, cats populate all the continents today.

Cats with Class

Taxonomists—the scientists interested in classifying everything—explain the scientific arrangement of domesticated cats like this:

> **Kingdom:** Animalia
>
> **Phylum:** Chordata
>
> **Class:** Mammalia
>
> **Order:** Carnivora
>
> **Family:** Felidae
>
> **Genus:** *Felis*
>
> **Species:** *silvestris*

The Earliest Known Pet Cat

While the ancient Egyptians have been widely credited with domesticating the cat roughly 4000 years ago, skeletal remains of an animal resembling a cross between a wild and a domesticated cat have been discovered that pre-date the Egyptian cat by several thousand years.

During a dig on the island of Cyprus, in the Mediterranean, archeologists found a 9500-year-old human grave. An assortment of worldly goods and the remains of an eight-month-old kitten were also found in the vicinity of the grave. The relationship between the animal and the human is unclear, but it appears the cat was purposefully and humanely laid to rest with the body.

No heaven will not ever be Heaven be; Unless my cats are there to welcome me.

–Unknown

Early Home Décor

Stone Age humans were probably very much like their modern-day counterparts when it came to sprucing up their accommodations. Bare cave walls became a canvas that ancient artists could decorate, along with other objects they created to enhance their living area. So it should be no surprise that engravings and pottery portraying cats, created as far back as 10,000 years ago, have been found.

Cat Art in Antiquity

Only bits of the murals that adorned the palace walls of Minoan Crete, circa 1600 BC, have survived the ravages of time. However, in one particular scene, a feline is behind a hedge planning an attack on a pheasant.

Another Greek artifact from the same era comes from a royal tomb at Mycenae—a bronze dagger with a blade that shows a cat hunting.

Décor in Life and Death

The nobles of Egypt lived and died surrounded by art. The remains of a wall painting in the tomb of Amenemheb show the privileged man hunting from his boat in a wetland area. His hunting cat clenches three birds in its paws and mouth.

When in Rome

The elite members of the Roman Empire spared no expense when it came to the materials used in their homes. Decorative mosaic tiles were used for flooring and walls. Tiles depicting hunting cats and their prey were discovered among the ruins in Pompeii, Italy, circa 1 AD.

Here Kitty, Kitty

Archaeological evidence reveals how important the cat was in ancient Egyptian culture. In fact, the ancient Egyptians can take credit for giving the modern world its favorite egocentric pet.

The quadruped predator protected the Egyptians' food storage from pests, and its hunting skills, among other endearing qualities, earned it iconic status.

FELINE GODS

Then They Were Gods

As cats gained favor and increased prominence within Egyptian culture, they became sacred and were celebrated in paintings and statues. Their rising glorification began to spread, resulting in an assortment feline deities, including Bastet.

The goddess Bastet, who resembled a cat, was also associated with fertility, music and dance.

Party Central

And, of course, a cat goddess requires a location where annual celebrations can be held in her honor.

A little town northeast of Cairo called Bast, later named Bubastis, became home of the yearly ritual of paying homage to Bastet. Folks gathered every year for outrageous parties that would make a college fraternity house bash look like a day-care—all in honor of Bastet.

Today, the temple is a mere shadow of its former glory as it lies in ruins at a location known as Tell Basta.

Till Death Do Us Part, and Then Some

So beloved was the Egyptian family cat, that its human keepers shaved their eyebrows as a form of mourning upon the untimely death of their pet. Many cats received special treatment even after their death.

For individuals of elevated social status, burial sometimes included mummification of not only the human and his or her pet cats but also mice for the felines to feast on in the afterlife.

In one particular tomb dating back to 1778 BC, there was evidence of several cat skeletons and milk dishes placed together.

Some elaborate tombs were decorated with paintings of cats doing usual cat things, such as sitting under chairs, eating and hunting with their masters. Also surviving the ravages of time are cat statues, which indicate that cats were well fed and decorated with jewelry, such as pectoral plates, ear and nose rings and collars.

CAT FACT In the late 19th century, a farmer in Egypt was cultivating virgin land and discovered 300,000 cat mummies. The cache of bodies was marketed to buyers as fertilizer.

Dressed for Death

The unique preservation process of a feline body was conducted in six steps. Priests would first remove the internal organs then fill the body with sand or mud.

Next, the body was positioned into a sitting pose and tightly wrapped with linen. The cloth-wrapped corpse would then be decorated with face paintings or other designs using black ink. The final step was natural dehydration.

Instant Industry

The demand for mummified dead cats outstripped the supply. The priesthood founded the niche business of providing worshippers with ready-made cat mummies.

DYING TO BE LOVED

Pet Graveyards

The number of cat cemeteries found in Egypt would rival that of tombs found in the Valley of Kings.

Renowned for offering bronze images to their cat gods, Egyptians also thought they would gain more favor from the gods by presenting mummified cats. Ironically, millions of cats were killed, mummified and buried in worship of Bastet.

Kitten Mills

The zeal for worshippers to demonstrate their faith by presenting a mummified cat to the gods likely launched humanity's first kitten mills.

Some Egyptian temples became catteries, producing thousands of kittens for mummification. This lucrative business shortened a cat's lifespan, as the age of a feline victim was two to four months old. They were rushed to their death (and the afterlife) by strangulation. Ironically, Egyptian household pet cats were spared from sacrificial duties, enabling kitten mills to flourish for many years.

Double Standards

During the time of feline worship and the offering of mummified cats in Egypt, it was also against the law to murder cats. The penalty for such a crime was death.

When the Persians went to war against the Egyptians more than 2500 years ago, the front line would attach live cats to their chest-protecting shields, knowing an Egyptian warrior would not risk harming a cat for fear of incurring the death penalty.

Their Halos Slipped

The time around the 10th century was a notorious period in cat history. As cultures swapped religions and beliefs, felines became linked with black magic and witches.

The Deadly Years

Cats were executed by the thousands in Europe because people believed that they were witches in disguise. A reprieve for cats came for a short duration after the Crusades, but the atrocities resumed and were even exported to North America with the Colonists.

Modern Adoration

All things old are new again, and cats have regained their crown and rightful place as creatures superior to humans.

A cat sees no good reason why it should obey another animal, even if it does stand on two legs.

–Sarah Thompson

MORE THAN THE SUM OF ITS PARTS

Walk the Walk

An amazing piece of engineering, the body of a cat possesses capabilities, beauty and athleticism that compel humans to wish we were felines. The mechanics of a cat's gait are unique and are responsible for the animal's sleek, elegant movements when walking. Cats move their front and back left paws at the same time, then both paws on their right side. They share this style of locomotion with camels and giraffes. Horses can also be trained to race in this fashion.

On Point

Cats and dogs are the only animals that walk on their tippy toes. Cats' paws are heavily padded, which helps the creatures move in stealth mode.

Flat out, a cat can go from 0 to 31 miles per hour, especially with an aggressor on its tail.

Southpaw

Cats can be right- or left-handed, or both. Forty percent of felines are southpaws, 20 percent are right-pawed, and the remaining 40 percent are ambidextrous.

Spring-Loaded

Cats can launch upwards onto an object that is several times their own height. Powerful thigh muscles catapult a feline from ground zero to the top of a bookcase faster than you can blink your eyes. Any extra weight that a cat has gained will hamper setting world records for the highest or quickest jump.

Three types of muscles—cardiac, involuntary and voluntary—contribute to a cat's agility, power and grace. There are more than 500 involuntary muscles in a cat's body.

This Little Piggy Went to Market

Generally cats have five toes on their front paws; however, only four are used for movement. The fifth toe is a dewclaw and resembles a human thumb. The back paws have four toes.

Too Many Piggies

Some cats have extra toes, a genetic trait known as polydactyly, which means "many fingers."

Centuries ago, sailors valued polydactyls for their climbing and hunting talents; as a result, these cats were commonly seen on ships.

Bone to Pick

Depending on the breed, or more specifically the number of toes and the length of the tail and spine, the number of bones in a cat's body ranges between 230 and 250. The average cat has about 244 bones—that's 30 more than humans have.

Pedicure Puss

Claws are useful, retractable extensions that serve a variety of purposes. They can be used for defense or aggression, hunting or escape. When kitty is taking 10 rounds out on your new couch, he's giving himself a pedicure. A cat's claws are similar in design to an onion, with many layers that he must try to file away on a scratching post or piece of furniture.

 CAT FACT The mainframe, or rib cage, of a cat has 13 pairs of ribs.

The Tale of the Tail

A cat's tail is a multitasking and multipurpose extension of its body that has a language all its own. More than a dozen positions translate into moods, social status, vigor and mental state. The tail also plays a role in balance—especially as your cat walks gingerly among your heritage china.

Wait Until Dark

The cat's ability to see in low light correlates with kitty's glow-in-the-dark eyes. Light reflects back from a layer of tissue, called the tapetum lucidum, hidden behind the eye's retina. It catches all the light that is not absorbed into the retina and directs it back inside so every speck of light is used. Combine that process with large corneas and pupils that dilate three times larger than those of humans and you have a predator with no need to learn braille.

Good Students Make Great Pupils
Cats' eyes control the amount of light that enters by reducing the pupils to vertical slits. A further adjustment to the volume of light entering the eye comes from eyelids that close at right angles. That's why you don't see cats with sunglasses.

 Ancient Egyptians believed that cats' eyes reflected the sun, even during darkness when the sun was down.

Third Eye...Lid
Working like a filter and moisturizer, a third eyelid, also called a haw, is neatly packaged in the corner of the eye.

The Nose Knows

Cats can almost smell that can of tuna before you bring it home from the store. Their olfactory power outranks that of humans by 30 times. The nose's interior structure membrane contains 200 million odor-sensitive cells that don't miss a thing.

No Cowhide Here
The skin cover on a cat's nose is referred to as leather.

Open Wide

Cats possess the ability to catch a whiff of something through their mouth. The Jacobson's organ is located on the roof of their mouth between the hard palate and the septum. A connection of secret passages, known as ducts, transmits scent from a gaping mouth into the nasal cavity.

Is that You I Smell?
When the Jacobson's organ is being activated, the look on the cat's face closely resembles open-mouthed disgust. The nasty look is called the "flehmen response" and is often seen when a tom catches a waft of air carrying the aroma of a female in heat.

Can You Hear Me Now?

Kittens are not born with the ability to hear; that sense takes about 14 days to develop. But when it does kick in and the ear canal opens, cats have superior hearing to humans. The frequency range of a cat's hearing ability beats out that of humans by three to one.

The sound-catching appendages signal a variety of moods, from relaxed or alert to defensive or aggressive.

Heavy Petting

The coat of a cat is made up of four different types of hair. The outer, coarser coat is guard hair. Moving inwards, the middle hair is called "awn" and the layer closest to the skin, which works like a pair of long johns, is "down." The fourth type makes up the whiskers.

Hair is 95 percent protein. Depending on its breed, and whether it has fine or coarse hair, a cat's body has from 7–22 hairs per pore, providing protection and warmth, not to mention plenty of hairball material.

That Tickles

We call them whiskers; science named them vibrissae. These custom-made hairs are sensitive to the world around kitty. They tell a cat whether or not she will fit through that opening in the fence. Of course if kitty puts on a few pounds, all bets are off. A cat's four rows of facial extensions are feelers, much like human fingers. If cats were poker players, their whiskers would be a "tell." When a cat's tactile hairs are in reverse, watch out, but if the whiskers face forward, it indicates either curiosity or just a good mood.

A Taste of Things to Come

Looking like a rasp because of the pebbly covering, called "papillae," a cat's tongue can tell whether or not you laced its food with medicine and can distinguish between salty, bitter, sweet and sour food items. The tongue is a primary tool for grooming, but the water-absorbent and highly mobile organ can also lap up fluids. Kittens lick things to explore their surroundings.

Feline Therapy

The ritual of a cat performing a solo, choreographed cleaning is called "autogrooming." When it becomes a group effort, it's referred to as "allogrooming." It may seem as if the cat suffers from obsessive-compulsive disorder when it comes to being clean, but grooming also helps to boost vitamin ingestion and to water-proof the cat's coat and improve its insulating abilities. Felines also groom after stressful situations and to reinforce or remove a scent. For this task, the tongue is like a therapist, only free.

Mealtime Hoovers

Sometimes it looks as if the cat inhaled that treat—that's because a cat can swallow and digest its food without having to chew it.

Straighten that Fur

As early as two weeks old, kittens learn from their mother to become neat freaks with their cleaning habits. Grooming dominates almost half of a cat's waking hours. The ritual of the body wash usually begins with the mouth, whiskers and chin. Next the cat moves on to the shoulders and the front legs. The flanks, genitals and tail round out the washing routine.

Of course, there are always a few felines that are not so high maintenance and don't devote much time to their appearance. Perhaps they prefer an edgier look, though neglecting their daily hygiene regimen can be a sign of illness.

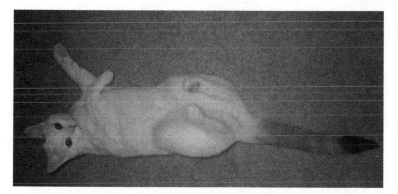

Gak Gak Goes the Cat

With all that grooming going on in between naps, a buildup of indigestible hair can accumulate in the stomach. There are only two exits. If the hairball takes the northern route, the hacking sound that comes out of the cat can make a person want to perform the Heimlich maneuver on the feline. That wet, gummy mass of hair and mucus that lands on your new carpet is called trichbezoar.

THE ART OF PURRING

Drone Power

Cats corner the market in the art of oral expression. Felines purr when they are content, birthing, in pain and even while they are dying. CSIs, or cat science investigators, don't fully comprehend the mechanics that enable some cats, such as household cats, ocelots and servals (not the larger cats such as tigers and lions) to purr. But there are a few schools of thought on how it occurs. Some experiments indicated that purring is a reflex caused by quick, rhythmic pressure changes in the windpipe. Another theory points to a set of false vocal chords. A different opinion suggests the purr comes from the vicinity of the hyoid bone in the throat.

Elephants make a sound that some people equate with a purr; however, elephant and big cat handlers Maureen Anderson and Brenda McComb at Edmonton's Storyland Valley Zoo say the sound is more like a rumble or flutter. The Asian elephant makes a rumbling noise from its upper sinus cavity, while the African elephant can create sound in its trunk and throat. Raccoons, too, have been known to make a sound that resembles a purr.

Cats purr while inhaling and exhaling, giving the listener a sense that the vocalization is nonstop. Elephants and raccoons do not display that talent.

The Power in the Purr

A study into the mystery of the purr draws a link to vibrational stimulation. Vibration has been found to relieve suffering in more than three-quarters of humans experiencing acute and chronic pain. Other benefits include new tissue growth, enhanced wound tissue strength, improved local circulation and oxygenation, a decrease in swelling and inhibition of bacteria growth.

Researchers used an accelerometer to measure the purr and the direction it traveled in the body. A study group of five cat species (domestic cat, cheetah, serval, puma and ocelot) was recorded for the examination. Frequency levels were between 20 Hz (one hertz equals one cycle per second) and 200 Hz.

Analysis indicates the levels were within very beneficial therapeutic parameters. At the end of a hard workout of playing, chasing and climbing, purring might be the equivalent of a moggie massage, and if an injury has occured, the vibrations may stimulate healing.

Do Re Mi

Cats produce roughly 60 to 100 different notes that vary in intensity from a gentle purr to a caterwaul that will have your neighbors running for earplugs.

FROM THE INSIDE OUT

Bloodlines

As early as 1912, it was presumed cats had blood groups. As more research was carried out, it was discovered that cats have A and B blood groups, and less than one-tenth of one percent has the rare AB blood type. An overwhelming 98 percent of non-pedigreed cats in the U.S. have Type A blood, with the remaining two percent having Type B. However, blood type percentages vary in other countries. Between 11 and 15 percent of cats in France and Italy have Type B. Some pedigreed felines tell a slightly different story. Up to 50 percent of British shorthair and Devon rex breeds have Type B blood.

After little more than two months of gestation, pregnant cats welcome a new batch of kittens. The average length of a normal pregnancy is between 58 and 72 days.

Check Your Pulse
The rhythmic beat of a cat's heart varies for each individual; however, the normal range for a resting feline is 160 to 240 per minute. Of course kittens can get a rise out of anything, including their pulse—spiking it much higher.

Holding a cat's wrist won't yield a pulse like it does in humans, but placing your fingers above the ribs behind the left elbow will.

Mercury Rising
The optimum body temperature for a cat is 101.5°F.

Don't Sweat It
The cooling system of a cat is unlike that of its owners. Attached to a cat's hair follicles are sac-like devices that release a milky type fluid, which catches the attention of a potential mate.

Situated in the cat's paws are sweat glands that operate similar to human sweat glands but far less efficiently. With little sweat evaporation possible, a cat relies on other methods, such as grooming, to cool off.

Lactose Intolerant?

After being weaned from their mother's milk, kittens don't require a substitute beverage other than fresh water, though some like drinking from mud puddles.

Cow's milk generally upsets their stomachs and results in a bad case of the runs. Some felines can tolerate milk without the side effects, but offering your cat his dinner without a bottle of white Château Dairy will save on paper towels.

Her world is an infinite shapeless white, 'til her tongue has curled the last holy drop.

–Harold Monro, from his poem "Milk for the Cat"

Just a Little Insurance

Most cat owners have a physician for their pet—the vet. And like medical attention that can be accessed at any time for humans, vets are available around the clock for feline medical emergencies in addition to normal business hours for routine checkups and other medical services.

Research has provided more treatments for feline ailments that ensure a successful outcome, but these can be costly. Medical insurance is available to help keep those vet bills down. For a monthly fee, many treatments are available for kitty that won't break the bank.

ABC's of Feline Disease

Although cats are amazing creatures, they like their human owners, can fall prey to disease and infection.

FeLV
Known in layman's terms as feline leukemia, this disease is the leading cause of cat deaths. A breakthrough vaccine can boost a cat's immune system against this fatal disease.

FIP
Feline infectious peritonitis is a debilitating disease, especially for kittens and senior cats. Scientists have designed a vaccine against it.

FUS
Not an infectious disease, feline urological disease is the formation of stones in the bladder or urethra. Some crystals can pass through the urinary system without notice; however, some can cause a blockage. Medicine along with diet or lifestyle changes can aid this plugging problem.

FIA

A blood parasite is the cause of feline infectious anemia. A regimen of antibiotics for 30 days suppresses the organism while allowing the cat to recover. Many cats, even though treated, remain carriers of the disease.

FIV

Feline immunodeficiency virus, while similar to the human form of AIDS, is not transmissible to people, only to other cats. There is no cure yet; however, a cat can be supported with treatment during the palliative stage. Death occurs within three years.

FCV

Vaccinations are available for feline calicivirus, an infection that invades the upper respiratory tract. This common disease can cause mild symptoms in one cat and severe signs in another.

Dementia

More people probably associate dementia with cat owners—those crazy cat ladies—rather than the mind thief known as Alzheimer's disease. Research indicates that aging cats can develop a similar form of the disease. But medical experts say a good diet, regular mental stimulation and companionship help keep dementia at bay in both humans and cats.

Eat It, Don't Smoke It

For carnivores, grazing on grass serves a number of purposes. Ingesting greenery can help dislodge hairballs to evacuate at either end or just provide a little dietary fiber. The folic acid found in your lawn also aids in the production of hemoglobin.

Weight Watchers

Obesity has spilled over into the world of felines. Feline health practitioners have devised a caloric intake formula that, when combined with exercise, should keep Fluffy from becoming flabby.

The daily energy requirement (DER) of an adult cat depends on a few factors such as its activity level and whether or not it is neutered. Neutering, for example, decreases the energy needs of an adult male by almost one-third. Adult cats require approximately 50 kcals for each pound of weight. Fat has the most calories, about 250 kcals an ounce, but we all know a steady diet of fat is not beneficial for cats (or humans). Carbohydrates and protein provide roughly 110 kcals per ounce.

Shape Up

Obese cats, like humans, are susceptible to an assortment of diseases. You can usually tell when your cat is too fat; however, body condition charts indicate just how portly your cat is. On an obese cat, the ribs and backbone are hard to see and feel, and the abdomen is well rounded with a barely visible to absent waistline. Its flabby folds can be seen swaying from side to side when the cat walks.

Hearing Deficit

Almost 50 percent of pure white cats with blue eyes are deaf. The problem lies with a defective dominant white gene. In some cases where a white cat has only one blue eye, the ear on the same side is hearing impaired.

The average indoor feline urinates twice a day and defecates once, while their outdoor living counterparts double up on bathroom duty.

I'd Rather Be Napping

Sleep, the sport of cats; well, at least the ones I own. A cat's waking hours make up roughly 30 percent of its entire life. That means a 15-year-old cat has probably slept for 10 of those years.

Foraging Habits

Feral cats typically dine between 10 and 20 times a day, with a lot of time spent searching out a meal. Duplicating this feeding behavior with indoor pet cats helps cut down on weight gain and inactivity. Ways to achieve ideal eating habits include the use of puzzle feeders, interactive toys and hiding food so the indoor feline can "hunt" for a meal.

Making a homemade puzzle feeder can be as simple as cutting holes in a plastic milk jug so that the cat can stick a paw inside to scoop out the food.

Dental Month

The American Veterinary Dental Society recognizes February as National Pet Dental Health Month. Their 2007 theme, "Flip the Lip," is a reminder to owners to be vigilant with their pets' teeth. Toothbrushes and specially formulated pet toothpaste should be in every pet owner's home to ward off bad kitty breath caused by plaque and tartar. But more importantly, according to pet dentists, lurking bacteria can be responsible for more serious health issues if left unchecked. If the cat won't let an owner anywhere near its mouth with a toothbrush, there are oral rinses available. Annual checkups by the dentist are also recommended. What about flossing?

Playing Doctor

Feline health practitioners recommend that cat owners play vet, cleaning their cat's ears and taking its temperature. This can help reduce kitty's stress during a real visit to the doctor.

The Predator Within

The urge to hunt is a learned behavior. If the mother cat is a non-hunter, the chance of the offspring being predatory decreases.

Behavior Modification

Some cats have undesirable behaviors, besides ignoring humans. After exhausting all attempts to rectify the behaviors and ruling out any medical causes for the problems, your vet can prescribe medications to treat ongoing issues such as cats that are overly fearful, aggressive or obsessive–compulsive.

Patterned after human medications, feline drugs work by altering specific neurochemical receptor functions, which can help to quell those anxiety attacks kitty may exhibit. Some of the meds include the drug classes of Paxil, Zoloft and Prozac.

MUTANT MOGGIES

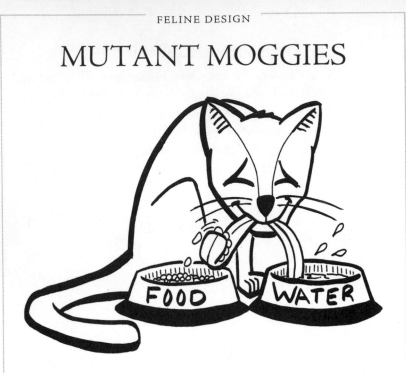

The Cat that Speaks with a Forked Tongue

Five Toes, a black shorthair from North Carolina, is so named because it has five digits on each paw. Alternative names the owner could have used for the cat's other unique body characteristic would be too tongue-in-cheek. Five Toes has two tongues. Owner Bill Whittington said people react with laughter when they hear about the double lapping devices—that is, until they see them.

Double Mug

A seven-year-old Massachusetts feline has defied the odds by surviving his unusual defect. Born with two faces, the cat with two names (Frank and Louise) was saved from being euthanized despite a bleak prognosis. The feline has two mouths, two noses and only two functional eyes.

It is extremely rare for a cat to be born with two faces, and death usually occurs within a few days.

Six Pack

The Hervey Foundation for Cats near Stony Plain, Alberta, had an unusual orange tabby at their sanctuary that required veterinarian attention. Willoughby was born with six legs and needed surgery to aid his mobility. An X-ray determined that the best course of action was to amputate two limbs on his torso's left side. According to Dr. Tammy Wilde, the vet who performed the operation at Tudor Glen Veterinary Clinic in St. Albert, Alberta, the limbs were "half the normal size, intertwined and protruding from his body in opposite directions." At first glance, the front legs looked like a single limb; however, the two legs were fused at the elbow. They were left intact.

Two hours after his successful surgery, Willoughby went home to recover with three strong legs. The tri-ped adapted well to the loss of his extra legs and is now very mobile. Marjorie Hervey says Willoughby is a remarkable cat that has made an extraordinary turnaround from being born deformed and abandoned to being rescued and then undergoing surgery. He has made great strides from the shy, frightened kitten he was when he arrived at the sanctuary to the funny character he is finally comfortable revealing.

CATS IN PRINT

The Cat that Outstayed His Welcome

The cat came back the very next day,
The cat came back, we thought he was a goner,
But the cat came back, he just couldn't stay away

Countless children and children's entertainers have sung that chorus of *The Cat Came Back* since Harry S. Miller wrote the song in 1893. The many verses tell the tale of Old Man Johnson and his farfetched and failed attempts to get rid of an unwelcome cat. The song was the catalyst for Cordell Baker to produce a short animated film of the same title in 1988.

That'll Learn Ya

Aesop, a Greek slave who died in 565 BC, is credited with creating many fables that were passed down orally through the centuries. He crafted his tales using animals as the characters and ended the story with a lesson. Some examples of his fables that involve felines include *The Cat and the Mice, The Cat, The Weasel and the Rabbit, The Eagle and the Cat* and *Venus and the Cat.*

The Fashionable Cat

Celebrating 50 years of whimsy is the much-loved story by Dr. Seuss. *The Cat in the Hat* is a skillfully crafted, triple meter, rhyming story about a cat that entertains two latchkey children in a most unusual way. This fictional feline appeared in five of Seuss' books, and the story was made into a full-length feature film in 2003 starring Mike Meyers.

From Bestseller to Cat Obituary

English writer Thomas Hardy had a deep attachment to his cats that, with a twist of writing fate, were the catalysts behind his leap into poetry.

His poetic obituary to one of his pets, "Last Words To a Dumb Friend," might not have been written if Hardy hadn't stopped writing novels after the public outcry that resulted from his frank portrayal of sexual attraction in *Tess of the d'Urbervilles* and *Jude the Obscure* near the turn of the 19th century.

Cheshire Cat

This character, with his mysterious grin, created in 1865 by Lewis Carroll in *Alice's Adventures in Wonderland,* is printed indelibly on the minds of readers of the famous piece of children's literature. The disappearing cat, which would grin for Alice, gets its name from an English saying "to grin like a Cheshire cat."

Swashbuckling Cat

Charles Perrault wrote many children's fairy tales, including *Puss in Boots* in 1697. The author didn't have to stretch his imagination when he gave the prime character cunning abilities. A cat named Puss was the only item bequeathed to a miller's youngest son upon the miller's death. Disappointed by his inheritance, the young man debated the cat's future. To avoid being turned into a fashion garment, Puss promised to provide the lad wealth in exchange for footwear and a bag. The strikingly handsome cat in his tall leather boots caught a variety of game in the bag and presented the prey to the king on behalf of his master. However, Puss referred to his master by a noble name that duped the king into believing the cat's owner was an important man. Eventually, Puss brokered a meeting between the king's daughter and the miller's son. And it was love at first sight for the young pair, who then lived happily ever after. Puss's character even made a cameo appearance in the movie *Shrek 2* in 2004.

Dick Who?

Dick Whittington and His Cat is a fictional story, based on a real person, in which a cat saves the day. Richard Whittington was Lord Mayor of London in 1397, and the legend about him and his cat sprang up 200 years after his death.

In the tale, Whittington is an impoverished lad who seeks his fortune in London, a place where the streets are lined with gold—or so he believes. Destitute and disillusioned, he is befriended by a wealthy merchant and put to work in the kitchen. Whittington acquires a cat to rid his dwelling of rats and is persuaded by the merchant to part with his feline, who is eventually sold to a rich king. Dick is paid a handsome sum for his sacrifice.

The real Richard Whittington was neither poor nor a cat owner. But a statue of the fabled Whittington's cat is in a prominent public place on Highgate Hill in London.

Physically Challenged

Mother Goose rhymes have entertained children for centuries, and in one particular farfetched piece of verse, a crooked man buys a crooked cat.

Kipling Cat

In *The Cat Who Walked by Himself,* which appeared in *The Just So Stories* in 1902, famous writer Rudyard Kipling created an endearing legend that explains why cats live with people. In the tale, all of the animals except the cat relinquish part of their "wildness" in exchange for care and protection from man, and in return the animals would provide servitude and friendship. A cat appears at the humans' cave and bargains with a woman for acceptance, saying, "I am not a friend, and I am not a servant. I am the Cat Who Walks by Himself, and I wish to come into your cave." They negotiate; however, the feline must come to a separate agreement with the man and his dog. The man tries to establish his dominance over the cat by demanding obedience. The cat agrees to abide by the request but only while inside the cave. Cat might have been thinking *You're not the boss of me* when he gives the dog the same answer. As a result of the cat's refusal to completely sell out, both man and dog dictate the future treatment of felines by humans and canines—the cat keeps his side of the bargain and retains his independence when away from man and dog.

Poor Business Skills

Beatrix Potter penned a story called *Ginger and Pickles* about a cat and dog that run an animal store. Ginger, the yellow tom and his partner Pickles, a terrier, have a problem with their accounts receivable and must close the doors to their business.

COMIC STRIP CHARACTERS

An Ideal Disguised as a Cat

Krazy Kat made its comic strip debut in 1910 and won the hearts of millions. Some may argue that *Krazy Kat* was one of the greatest comic cats of all time. While George Herriman's creation was not a huge commercial success, it did have a loyal following, including U.S. President Woodrow Wilson. Herriman was often called a literary genius. The publication of *Krazy Kat* stopped on the death of Herriman in 1944.

Heathcliff

This comic strip anti-hero was the creation of George Gately and appeared in 700 papers during Heathcliff's rise to fame from 1973–81. His character, a macho guy with an understated manner, shares the name of Emily Bronte's primary character in *Wuthering Heights*. Heathcliff branched out to film and books.

Whose Cats?

Kliban's Cats—a motley crew of bizarre characters—can be found on everything from calendars, stationary and cards to bed sheets, purses and housewares since their debut in 1975. Kliban had four cats that he shared his home with and likely got his twisted sense of humor from them.

Three Decades of Antics

Created by Al Smith, *Cicero's Cat* first appeared in the newspaper funny section in 1933. Esmeralda, the black-striped feline star of the strip, outsmarted a variety of animals in her 30-year career.

Lasagna Lover

As Garfield, the closest thing to a human in fur, approaches 30 years of age, he will likely end up with the most beloved cat cartoon award—if he has anything to say about it. Creator Jim Davies named the colorful character after his grandfather. Garfield has appeared in 700 newspapers, books and animated TV shows. Garfield's favorite movie is *Old Yeller* and his least favorite food is raisins.

> *Show me a mouser and I'll show you a cat with bad breath.*
> –Garfield

Secret Cult Status

Fritz the Cat achieved fame in underground comics created by Robert Crumb during the 1960s. They were not your child-friendly weekend funnies. The incorrigible cat had a potty mouth and an appetite for the ladies. Fritz raised eyebrows when he appeared in the first x-rated animated film, simply named *Fritz the Cat* and produced by Ralph Bakshi. Crumb tried to get the courts to block the release of the film but failed. His only chance to annihilate any possible sequel was for Fritz to "have an accident." Crumb produced a farewell strip in which Fritz was murdered by an unstable ostrich.

CATS ON STAGE AND SCREEN

Can I Have Your Autograph?

Cats were not content to stay in print and, through the talent and imagination of their creators, felines have found their way into the hearts and funny bones of film and TV audiences all over the world.

Ode to Kitties

Mike Smith, who plays the cat-loving character Bubbles in *The Trailer Park Boys* TV sitcom, has written and performed a song about kitties. One verse is dedicated to Vince the Pince, a cat born with two front paws that resemble a lobster's claw.

Bubbles, Vince and the rest of the cats that associate with Julian and Ricky in the fictional Sunnyvale Trailer Park often steal the show.

Dueling Duo

Tom and Jerry have played the cat and mouse game for nearly seven decades since MGM featured the pair in the cartoon *Puss Gets the Boot* in 1939. *Tom and Jerry* was the brainchild of Fred Quimby, William Hanna and Joseph Barbera. The animated enemies earned seven Oscars for their creators, and the cat and mouse made regular appearances in comic books and on television between 1942 and 1972.

Saved by a Whisker (and got rich, too)

Morris, the finicky eater in 9-Lives cat food commercials, was saved from death row at a shelter in 1968. Animal trainer Bob Martwick was hunting for talent for his next production and spied a Hollywood natural in the orange moggy. Martwick paid the five-dollar bail and sprang Morris into stardom. Though he appeared in the movie *Shamus* with Burt Reynolds and Dyan Cannon and he pawed a bill at the White House, Morris remained a humble cat. There have been four Morris cats since the inception of the commercial.

Across the Pond

The British equivalent of Morris was Arthur. His shtick was scooping food out of a tin with his paw. Arthur became a pawn in a two-year custody battle between Spillers, the pet food company who claimed they paid for ownership, and the cat's former owner.

At the beginning of the court case, Arthur vanished. When the former owner was sentenced for contempt of court, the feline resurfaced and was restored to the guardianship of Spillers. The former owner lost his case.

Arthur appeared in 309 commercials between 1966 and 1975 and marketed t-shirts and other paraphernalia. He died in 1976, just shy of his 17th birthday.

Sufferin' Succotash!

Warner Brothers brought I. Friz Freleng's animated black and white "puddy tat" to life on the silver screen in 1945. Sylvester spent his life trying to outwit, then dine on Tweety Pie, a yellow canary. Sylvester's talent earned Freleng two Oscars.

Perennial Favorite

Felix the cat began his career in the movies in 1917 and then moved to comics in 1923. Cartoonist Pat Sullivan's debut of Felix in a short animated film beat out Walt Disney's introduction of another black and white animal, Mickey Mouse, by almost a decade.

The World of Walt

Whether child, parent or grandparent, Disney's animated films are a steady diet for movie fans. Cats have played both starring and supporting roles in several of the classics.

Disney Diva

In the *Aristocats,* Duchess, a Parisian mother cat, and her kittens are catnapped by the butler, who fears he will lose out on an inheritance that will become his only after the passing of the cats. Duchess befriends a trio of characters that assist her and the kittens to return home and bust the butler for his scheming. You'll have to watch the movie to see how it turns out.

Mother's Little Helper

Lucifer's character in *Cinderella* was the antagonist and rotten, child-like pet of the wicked stepmother. Lucifer did what cats do—chased mice. But in this case, the mice were Cinderella's ill-treated friends and helpers. Their ongoing battle is part of the good-versus-evil plot in the classic Disney animated fairy tale film.

He's Not the Barber

In Walt Disney's feature length classic *Pinocchio,* which debuted in 1940, the wooden puppet's father, Gepetto, owned a cat named Figaro.

Sneaky Siamese

A pair of spoiled Siamese makes life miserable for Lady in *Lady and the Tramp* when they arrive with Aunt Sarah to housesit. Si and Am leave a trail of mischief as they wind their way up the stairs towards the baby's room. When Lady barks to alert Aunt Sarah of the impending danger the cats pose, the felines feign injury, and Lady gets the blame.

All the Alley's a Stage

One of the most successful musical plays of the 20th century features humans pretending to be felines. *Cats* composer Andrew Lloyd Webber adapted T.S. Eliot's book *Old Possum's Book of Practical Cats* to music, and after several years of tinkering and collaboration, the musical play made its debut in 1981 to rave reviews. The winner of numerous awards, *Cats* has played in theaters around the world and has been translated into several languages.

REAL CATS IN REEL MOVIES

Sometimes Hollywood just uses the word cat in its titles; however, knowing the movie public love their felines, film producers have included many cats in their casts, even giving them starring roles in full-length features.

The Black Cat—released in 1934; a scary movie based on Edgar Allen Poe's story of the same name

The Case Of the Black Cat—a Perry Mason murder mystery produced in 1936

The Black Cat—released in 1941; a murder mystery starring Basil Rathbone

Cat People—this 1942 horror movie involved a girl that could transform into a deadly panther

The Curse of the Cat People—of course, you knew there had to be a sequel; released in 1944

Rhubarb—released in 1951; a comedy starring Ray Milland as a wealthy man who bequeaths everything he owns, including his baseball team, to his ginger cat, Rhubarb

Bell, Book and Candle—a 1958 comedy about a witch and her cat

Breakfast at Tiffany's—a ginger tom named Cat played a supporting role in this 1961 romantic comedy

Shadow of the Cat—in this 1961 who-dun-it, the cat solves the mystery of who killed its owner and metes out justice

The Incredible Journey—a 1964 Disney feature; follows the trail of a trio of animals, which includes a Siamese cat, as they face a variety of challenges on their way home

One Day, A Cat—a 1963 Czechoslovakian fantasy film that involves a cat wearing bifocals

The Three Lives of Thomasina—a Disney classic, released in 1963, about the cat of a veterinarian's daughter

That Darn Cat—a 1965 comedy about a cat that helps to catch a group of bank bandits

The Night of the Thousand Cats—a 1972 Mexican-produced horror flick featuring man-eating cats that liked young women on the menu

Harry and Tonto—an unforgettable 1974 drama that earned Art Carney an Oscar for playing an elderly widower who takes a journey with his pet cat Tonto after being evicted from his apartment

The Uncanny—a 1977 Canadian trilogy of stories about evil cats

The Cat from Outer Space—a 1978 Disney flick about a super smart, extraterrestrial cat stuck on earth

Our Johnny—a 1980 Austrian production about the effect a cat has on the lives of a family

Cat People—a 1982 remake of the 1942 classic; stars Nastassia Kinski and Malcolm McDowell as the lone survivors of an ancient tribe of leopard-humans

Cat's Eye—a three-in-one horror 1985 flick, starring Drew Barrymore; a cat tries to save a young girl from supernatural danger

Pet Sematary—the 1989 adaptation of a Stephen King novel; a family's cat and young son come back to life to wreak havoc on a small town after being buried in the local cemetery

Cats & Dogs—a 2001 film about the top-secret, high-tech struggle between two eternal enemies

Parody Pussycat

Hollywood and television actress Mary Tyler Moore owns a television production company called MTM whose logo is a kitten mewing, a comical take on the famous movie production company Metro-Goldwyn-Mayer's roaring lion.

A meow massages the heart.

–Stuart McMillan

LITERARY CATS

Many people are smitten with kittens, and famous folks are no exception. They, too, fall prey to the charms of felines. Of note is the fascination writers have with cats, not only in their poetry, plays and stories but also those under their care.

Nanny Kitty

American novelist and Nobel and Pulitzer Prize recipient, Ernest Hemingway adored and treasured his feline companions. Because Hemingway had such unwavering faith in cats, he allowed F. Puss, his golden-eyed pet cat, to mind his sleeping infant child in the crib.

Wherever Hemingway lived, including in his home in Key West, Florida, many cats could be found under his care. Descendents of the colony of polydactyls he owned while residing in the tropical paradise can still be found at his home-turned-museum.

One cat just leads to another.

–Ernest Hemingway

Family Heirloom

Charlotte Brontë, who penned *Jane Eyre,* and her sister Emily Brontë of *Wuthering Heights* fame shared and spoiled a cat named Tiger. While in Brussels, Charlotte wrote to her sister and expressed her yearning to be at home feeding the best part of a lamb dinner to Tiger.

Authors like cats because they are such quiet, loveable, wise creatures, and cats like authors for the same reasons.

–Robertson Davies

 Lord Byron, author of *Don Juan,* had five cats that were also his traveling companions.

Intoxicated by Felines

Rudyard Kipling, who gave us *The Jungle Book,* embodied his feelings about cats with words from the story of the same name, "He will kill mice and he will be kind to babies…but when the moon gets up and the night comes, he is the Cat Who Walks by Himself…"

Turn-of-the-Century Humor

Edward Lear acquired Foss, a striped male kitten, in 1873. An employee chopped off Foss' tail to keep him from roaming, and in Lear's published drawings, the cat sports his new look. Lear so loved his cat that when they moved into a new residence, Lear had the interior renovated to look exactly like the old place. He didn't want Foss to have any problems adjusting to the new location.

Don't Forget to Check Your Spelling

You have heard of backseat drivers—how about a backseat writer? Henry James often wrote with a cat perched on his shoulder. James' titles includes *The Bostonians* and *Portrait of a Lady.*

Who Done It?

Mystery writer Raymond Chandler, creator of the character
Philip Marlowe, had a black Persian assistant that he would read
his first drafts to.

Lazy is as Lazy Does

While in exile on the British island of Guernsey, French novelist
Victor Hugo, known for *Les Miserables* and *The Hunchback of Notre
Dame*, had an Angora companion named Gavroche. However, the
cat was deemed lethargic in nature so he was renamed Chanonine—
a French phrase that loosely translates to mean "to live an easy life."

It's Not What You Say, But How You Say It

Samuel Johnson, the 18th-century writer also known for his lex-
icography skills, would go to the market to purchase oysters for
his pampered cat Hodge. Johnson was under the illusion that his
cat could read his mind as well as understand his comments.
Johnson once said that he had owned better cats than Hodge,
but he backpedaled on his statement because he thought it
caused Hodge displeasure.

Rack 'Em Up

Mark Twain, a.k.a Samuel Clements, was so devoted to his cats that he rewrote the house rules when playing pool to allow the felines to interfere with a moving ball on the billiard table.

If man could be crossed with the cat it would improve man, but it would deteriorate the cat.

–Samuel Clements

Eulogy for a Feline

English writer Thomas Hardy was so brokenhearted when his cat died that he wrote an obituary in rhyme, proclaiming never to own another. Years later, he relented when given a Persian he dubbed Cobby. The pair was inseparable until Hardy's death in 1928, at which time Cobby disappeared. What follows is a bizarre and unconfirmed explanation of Cobby's whereabouts.

Hardy's executor, Sir Sydney Cockerell, wanted Hardy to be buried at Poet's Corner in Westminister Abbey, but his friends and family preferred to lay him to rest in the same grave as his wife in the village of Stinsford. As a compromise, the two parties decided to have an urn containing Hardy's ashes buried at Poet's Corner and his heart buried in the village. A physician removed the heart and placed it in a biscuit tin next to the body. Since Cobby had been Hardy's constant companion, it is alleged that he chose to be near the body and managed to open the container and eat part of the heart. When discovered the next day by the undertaker as the proverbial cat that ate the canary, Cobby was strangled, then placed in the tin to be buried in the village.

From Supernatural Stories to a Cat Elegy

H.P. Lovecraft, American writer of horror and supernatural fiction, wrote an eight-line epitaph to his beloved pet cat Oscar after the feline was killed by a vehicle.

A Feline Heating Pad

Edgar Allen Poe owes the creation of his short, dark tale *The Black Cat* to his shorthaired critter, Catarina. The delightful cat provided comfort and warmth to Poe's tuberculosis-stricken wife during the last year of her life. Living in poverty, Mrs. Poe used her husband's coat and the tortoiseshell cat to keep warm while bed-ridden during her final winter.

The Power of the Paw

It is not known whether Charles Dickens was penning *A Christmas Carol* or one of his other well-known classics when his cat gave birth to kittens. He decided not to keep the litter, but one of the tiny felines caught his eye, so he allowed her to stay. The little female, which he named Master's Cat, liked the attention received from Dickens so much that she would put out the reading candle with her nimble paw to get noticed.

Covert Cats

Anne Frank, the diarist who would become a symbol of Jewish suffering during World War II, had three cats while hiding from the Nazis. The young teenager and her family were concealed in an Amsterdam warehouse attic, where two of the cats were living before their arrival. The third cat came with another family seeking refuge from persecution.

Poets generally love cats—because poets have no delusion about their superiority.

–Marion Garretty

Shaken Not Stirred

One of the cats belonging to writer T.S. Eliot was christened Noilly Prat, also the name of a brand of vermouth.

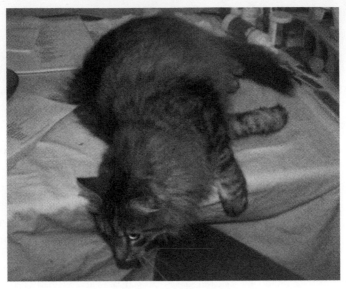

Can I Lick the Spoon?

George Sand, the pen name of Aurore Dudevant, was unusually close to her cat Minou. The pair ate their breakfast from the same bowl.

La Chat Mania

Often attributed with creating a large fan base for cats among French writers and intellects during the 19th and 20th centuries, Sidonie Gabrielle Colette penned stories with cat characters inspired by her pets. Her passion for felines spilled into her literary work *La Chatte,* which tells the story of a cat whose owner leaves his wife because the woman is mean to the cat.

> *Making friends with a cat can only be*
> *a profitable experience.*
>
> –Sidonie Gabrielle Colette

A Cat Named for a Poem

Argentinian author Jorge Luis Borges had a cat called Beppo, named after a poem written by Lord Byron.

OTHER CAT COMPANIONS

Guess Who's Coming to Dinner?

Sir Winston Churchill shared his dinner table with his cat, Jock. If Jock failed to show for mealtime, Churchill would not begin eating until the cat was rounded up by servants and sitting at the table. Jock was included in Churchill's will.

The wartime prime minister, who resided at No. 10 Downing Street in London, held his cats—and he had several of them throughout his life—in the highest regard.

As a strange aside, Churchill's political confidant was named Mr. Kat.

Spiritual Roots

Historically, cats have been linked with spirituality and faith, so it should not come as a surprise to learn that Muhammad had a cat. According to legend, the Muslim prophet once cut the sleeve off his garment so as not to disturb a cat snoozing on his arm.

The Cat Lady with the Lamp

Florence Nightingale, pioneer of nursing, not only tended to wounded soldiers in the Crimean War but also owned 60 cats in her lifetime.

Preferring the Company of Cats

Charles Baudelaire was known for his bold poems and his obsession for cats. His attentiveness to cats instead of his companions caused much uproar. When visiting someone's home for the first time, Baudelaire would be fidgety and impatient around the humans until he met the homeowner's cat, at which time he would smother the animal with lavish affection while ignoring the humans.

Art Imitating Life
Pablo Picasso, the Spanish artist who is associated with the cubism movement, depicted cats in his work in an unusual style and form. In some of his paintings, the cats look like they were reassembled with their body parts rearranged. Despite the unusual artistry Picasso displayed on canvas, the cats that shared his home were very ordinary.

Purrs and Pianos
Domenico Scarletti was a 17th-century Italian composer who received a little help from his cat Pulcinella. The feline commonly walked back and forth across the harpsichord keyboard. A sequence of notes the cat created led Scarletti to arrange a piece that became known as *The Cat's Fugue in G minor.* The composer shared the credit with Pulcinella.

Animal Activist
French film star Brigitte Bardot devoted herself to animal welfare after retiring from the movies. Aside from setting up a foundation for the welfare and protection of animals that offers a spay and neuter program for feral cats in France, she shelters 60 stray cats in her home.

There's a Sucker Born Every Minute
Phineas Taylor Barnum was known for his attractions, for which Americans would pay money to see. During the late 1800s, P.T. Barnum claimed to have a cherry-colored cat for exhibit. Cat fanciers and other curious people came in droves to see the red feline. To their dismay and anger, they paid to view a black cat. The showman's reply to their demands for a refund was that some cherries are black.

The Cat That Didn't Come Back

Sir Ernest Shackleton is best known for his Antarctic expedition in 1914, not for the feline crewmember he ordered to be shot.

Mrs. Chippy, a macho tabby tomcat was originally from Glasgow, Scotland, and belonged to Henry McNeish, a master shipwright. The pair set sail from London heading to the South Pole on Shackleton's ship, the *Endurance,* on August 1.

About six weeks into the trip Mrs. Chippy used up one of his lives by making a break for freedom and jumping through a porthole. He landed in the frigid, dark water of the south Atlantic, and the ship's watchman heard the pleading mews and turned the ship around for a rescue.

Mrs. Chippy settled back into his routine as they continued their passage to the Antarctic. In January 1915, the *Endurance* became trapped in ice despite attempts to free her. By the time October rolled around, all hope of freeing the ship from the captive ice diminished. The crew's only option for survival was to walk 350 miles through the desolate and harsh environment to land. The journey would be treacherous, and the men were ordered to minimize the essentials they would have to carry. Mrs. Chippy did not join the search for land; instead Shackleton made the decision to put him down. The crew said their good-byes to the cat individually before making the arduous expedition, and Mrs. Chippy became a martyr to the cause of polar exploration. Miraculously, the crew made it out, but McNeish never forgave Captain Shackleton for the loss of his cat.

In 2004, a bronze sculpture of Mrs. Chippy was placed on the final resting place of McNeish in New Zealand.

Cats are smarter than dogs. You can't get eight cats to
pull a sled through snow.

–Jeff Valdez

PRESIDENTIAL CATS

Martha's Cats

The White House in Washington, D.C., has seen its fair share of cats, starting with the Washingtons. First Lady Martha had a cat door installed at Mount Vernon to accommodate the whims of her cats.

Two-Term Cats

Theodore Roosevelt, president from 1901 to 1909, was a cat supporter who had a polydactyl cat named Slippers and a trickster kitten named Tom Quartz. Roosevelt recorded the antics of Tom Quartz in a letter to his son; apparently the American president yielded to Slippers when the feline refused to budge from a spot on the floor that blocked the passage of the president and his guests to another room in the White House.

Historical Gift

Rutherford Hayes, the 19th president, served from 1877 until 1881 and is credited for importing the first Siamese to the U.S. The U.S. consul in Bangkok presented the kitten as a gift for First Lady Lucy Hayes.

From the Governor's Mansion to the Oval Office

It was a black and white kitten that picked Governor Bill Clinton's daughter Chelsea in 1991. Two kittens were playing in the yard of Chelsea's music teacher, and when the young Clinton knelt down, Socks—as he was christened—jumped into her arms.

When Bill Clinton made the leap to Washington, Socks, now well entrenched in the family's lives, also went along. The press fawned over the feline, snapping photos for the papers. The presidential cat was included in political life with visits to schools and nursing homes. Life threw Socks a curve when Chelsea went to college and President Clinton acquired a black lab pup named Buddy.

Socks never accepted Buddy, a high-energy pain in the cat's butt. Near the end of Clinton's second term, the cold war between the animals was solved when Socks was placed with a longtime Clinton employee, which worked well for everyone. The media-wary cat made a public appearance in 2005 at Andrews Air Base and was reported to still be in good health in mid-2006.

There is, incidentally, no way of talking about cats that enables one to come off as a sane person.

–Dan Greenberg

Other Presidential Flashbacks

- President Lincoln's son had a tabby; the American leader was also fond of cats.
- At the time of his assassination in 1901, William McKinley, a Republican president, was the owner of an Angora cat.
- The Kennedys had a cat but were forced to find it a new home because of the president's allergy to felines.
- The Fords had a Siamese, as did the Carters, which was named Misty Malarky Ying Yang.
- President Ronald Reagan was fond of animals but kept his cats out of the White House.
- President George W. Bush had cats in Texas, but only India went to live in Washington.

MORE FAMOUS CAT OWNERS

Diplomatic Kitty

From her humble beginnings in rural Saskatchewan to a high-profile career in the Big Apple, Pamela Wallin is better known as a broadcaster-turned-Canada's-consul-general to the United States than as a cat owner.

Wallin's Siamese, named Kitty, is the only thing that slows the pace of the ambitious and workaholic Canadian. Wallin has spent many a night's rest on a chair because she didn't want to disturb Kitty, who was sleeping on her lap.

There are few things more heartwarming in life than to be welcomed by a cat.

–Tay Hohoff

California, Here I Come

Actor James Mason brought a group of mainly Siamese cats to Hollywood when he relocated from England, and he wrote a book about his household cats that included his sketches. The neighborhood in Los Angeles where Mason and his wife lived had other famous Hollywood residents with a penchant for felines. They included Katherine Hepburn, Fred Astaire, Charlie Chaplin, Lucille Ball and Van Heflin.

Cats seem to go on the principle that it never does any harm to ask for what you want.

–Joseph Wood Krutch.

What Goes Out Must Come In

The man historians describe as "one of the greatest names in the history of humanity," Sir Isaac Newton wasn't all mathematics, physics and astronomy. The bachelor English scientist was a cat owner who eventually tired of interrupting his studies to let the feline in and out. Newton came up with a solution that is still popular today—the cat flap.

Oils or Watercolors?

Swiss painter Paul Klee surrounded himself with cats and included them in his paintings. His adoration of felines spawned an entire book, *The Cosmic Cats of Paul Klee*, written by Marina Alberghini, which highlighted his passion in life and work.

Cats know how to obtain food without labor, shelter without confinement and love without penalties.

–W.L. George

The Cat is a Ham

After a televised National Hockey League game between Edmonton and Calgary, CBC was interviewing Flames captain Jerome Iginla. It was an opportunity to talk about the game and review an earlier interview with Iginla's grandfather.

The clip showed a proud grandfather talking about his grandson's athletic abilities and some childhood history. About midway through the interview, the family cat jumped up beside the grandfather and started poking his head with a paw. Grandpa kept his cool and continued talking while the cat was swatting the top of his head. After several minutes of the cat trying to get the grandfather's attention and stealing the show, everyone erupted in laughter and the interview wrapped up.

The happiest houses are those in which kitten-bearing is held over as a permanent attraction.

–James Mason

FELINE PHOBIAS

Bitter and Jitters Over Fur-Clad Critters
It may be hard to fathom, but some people don't like cats, and others are scaredy-cats when it comes to felines. Some members of the anti-cat club may seem obvious, while others may come as a surprise.

Napoleon I
A kitten reportedly gave Napoleon Bonaparte, the French Emperor and brilliant militarist, the fright of his life. An aide responding to frenzied shouting in Bonaparte's bedroom found the Emperor in a state of hysteria, violently swinging his sword at a kitten hiding behind the drapes.

Go Look it up in the Dictionary
The American who gave us *Webster's Dictionary*, Noah Webster was not fond of felines and had this to say about them, "deceitful animal and when enraged, extremely spiteful."

Shoot First, Ask Questions Later
Dwight D. Eisenhower, American president and World War II hero, was not a fan of cats. He ordered his staff to shoot any felines that wandered onto his property.

It Takes Two to Tango
Famed founder of modern dance, American Isadora Duncan, was annoyed when cats from a neighboring sanctuary would defecate in her garden in Neuilly, France. She instructed her staff to capture the offending cats and drown them.

Anti-Cat Campaigner
If Chicago banker Rockwell Sayre had his way, the Roaring Twenties would have been purr-less. He started a crusade to rid the world of cats by 1925, offering 10 cents for each dead cat and $100 to the person responsible for killing the last remaining cat on earth.

Smelling Salts, Please

Henry III, the king of France in the 16th century, was not a macho man. He would pass out at the sight of a cat. He sent 30,000 cats to their deaths during his reign.

Catatonic

Alexander the Great conquered many things, but not his fear of cats. He was educated by Aristotle in 343 BC and had an affinity towards animals; however, the sight of a cat caused the mighty warrior to faint.

All Hail Kitty

Rome's greatest leader in ancient history was disgusted by felines. The sight of a cat repulsed Emperor Julius Caesar.

Playing William Tell with Cats

German composer Johannes Brahms didn't have a Zen garden to reduce stress in his life; instead, he hunted the neighborhood cats from an open window of his home with a bow and arrow for relaxation.

Those who dislike cats will be carried to the cemetery in the rain

–Dutch proverb

CAT WORDS

CAT: An acronym for a few things, including clear air turbulence, computerized axial tomography and computer-aided trading.

Cat and Fiddle: Many a watering hole or tavern has christened its premises with this name, which also appears in a child's nursery rhyme. The phrase originates from "Caton le fidele" (Caton the faithful), governor of Calais, France.

Cat and mouse: Another name for the game of tic-tac-toe

Catbird seat: A position of power, or a situation in which you have an edge over your opponent or competitor

Catboat: Broad across the beam, this sailboat has a single sail on a forward-stepped mast

Cat burglar: A term used for thieves—with nerves of steel—who scale tall buildings to commit crimes

Catcall: Every performer has a story of being the recipient of a catcall from a member of the audience. It is a noise that expresses impatience or dislike. Hiss, hiss, boo.

Catfight: A fight between two women

Catgut: Ironically, this thin, dried cord used as surgical thread and for stringing rackets and musical instruments doesn't come from cats, but from the intestines of sheep or other animals.

Cathead: The horizontal beam sticking out from the ship's bow that carries the anchor

Cat hole: A sailor's term for the two holes located at the stern of the ship through which large ropes are passed

Cat house: Another name for a bordello or house of ill repute (the working house of prostitutes). Since the 15th century, sex trade workers have been also labeled cats.

Catkin: An elongated bunch of small leaves and petal-less flowers that can be found on willows, birches and alders

Catnap: Sleep experts have coined this term for a brief snooze

Cat o' nine tails: An ancient tool of torture and punishment, it is a whip with nine strands of knotted rope and was frequently used to flog prisoners.

Cat rig: This is exactly what is implied, the rig of a catboat

Cat's cradle: A children's game in which string or yarn is looped around the fingers of one person and passed to another, changing the pattern with each pass

Cat's-eye: A child's playing marble with a splash of color at the center; a reflective unit embedded into a highway surface to alert drivers of lane boundaries; or a gem, such as chalcedony, that reflects a narrow band of light.

Cat's paw: A person duped into doing an unpleasant or distasteful task. The term comes from Aesop's fable in which a monkey encourages a cat to use his paw to retrieve hot roasted chestnuts from the fire.

Cat's pajamas: A term used to indicate that something is special. This term has been around for several centuries and refers to an English tailor by the name of E.B. Katz, who was known for producing elegant silk pajamas for the upper class. "Cat's meow" is another expression meaning the same thing.

Catsuit: A one-piece, snug-fitting garment, also called a body suit

Cattery: Another term for a cat-breeding establishment or a boarding facility for felines

Catty: A term used to describe someone who is covertly spiteful or malicious

Catwalk: A runway where top models strut their stuff; also a narrow walkway high above the stage in a theater

Kitty-corner: A term used to describe objects or places located on diagonal corners

CAT SAYINGS

Hold Your Tongue

The expression "Cat got your tongue?" is an everyday response to someone who does not reply while engaged in conversation. It became a popular expression in the 1800s. Legend has it that during the practice of removing the tongues of liars, the body part was then fed to cats.

Playing the Field

A female cat in heat may mate with several males, resulting in the street term "catting around."

That Rings a Bell

A situation or problem that can be resolved may be compared to "belling the cat." The expression stems from an old folk tale in which mice gathered to cook up a plan to get rid of the cat. After much debate, they decided to attach a bell to the cat's neck, which would warn them of approaching danger.

Smile and Say "Cheese"

"Grinning like a Cheshire cat" has more to do with cheese and swordsmen than a picture-posing feline. Early reference to this saying comes from a type of cheese made in Cheshire, England. The mold used in cheese production left an imprint of a grinning cat face without the body, creating the illusion that all but the grin had disappeared, much like the Cheshire cat in Lewis Carroll's famed *Alice in Wonderland*.

Another source for the expression dates further back, to around 1483, during the reign of King Richard III. Back then, folks would say "to grin like a Caterling" because of an infamous swordsman who would get a villainous smirk on his face before lunging with his sword. How "to grin like a Caterling" turned into "grinning like a Cheshire cat" is anyone's guess.

It's in the Bag

"To let the cat out of the bag" is to give away a secret. The expression stems from an old deception used at the marketplace. A cat was placed in a bag and sold as a pig. The switch would become apparent when the bag was opened.

Close Quarters

"Not enough room to swing a cat" is an expression that dates back to when the "cat o' nine tails" was used for punishment on sailing vessels. Whoever was meting out the punishment had to find a location where there would be enough room to swing the lengthy whip. The slash marks left from a flogging closely matched the damage inflicted by the claws of a wild feline.

A Theory that's All Wet

"Raining cats and dogs" is a metrological expression that describes a heavy rain. Some suggest that this expression came about because when towns with poor drainage flooded after heavy rainstorms, townfolk would see the narrow streets littered with the dead bodies of cats and dogs, and uneducated residents believed the animals had fallen from the sky.

Are You Ready to Rumble?

"To fight like Kilkenny cats" is an old Irish saying that means to brawl until there is only one survivor. The expression came about from a story of a group of soldiers who tied two cats together by their tails and hung them over a wire to watch them scrap. One serviceman had a change of heart and wanted to release them but could only do so by chopping off their tails. The cats bolted for freedom and the soldier was left holding the appendages when an officer arrived. When questioned about the activity and the contents in his hand, the soldier lied. He said the cats fought so savagely that all that remained was their tails.

FELINE FOLK WISDOM

You Can Lead Them to Water

When in France, make sure you don't cross a babbling brook carrying a cat. It's considered bad luck.

Think Pink

The outside walls of most northern homes have insulation, but it doesn't ward off bad spirits, just nasty winters. Centuries ago, in a region of England, it is said that mummified cats were placed within the walls of houses to keep away evil ghosts.

It's Not Just Black or White

Good luck in Scotland comes in the form of a strange black cat sitting on your porch.

In Ireland, death by illness was your fate if, on a moonlit night, a black cat crossed your path.

Some believed a black cat walking towards you meant good luck, but if it was heading in the opposite direction, it would take your good luck away.

Legend tells us that the king of England, Charles I, believed his black cat was lucky. Charles was so paranoid about losing the cat that he placed it under 24-hour surveillance. The day after the cat died, the king was arrested.

Students in England believed that seeing a white cat on their way to school spelled trouble. To have a trouble-free day, they would spit, spin around and make the sign of the cross.

During the 16th century, in England, visitors would kiss the family cat to leave good luck. The color of the feline didn't matter.

Cat-choo

Residents of Italy welcomed a sneezing cat because it was a good omen. Other European cultures believed that if a cat sneezed three times in a row, the owner would come down with a cold.

Tattle Tails

Families in Holland believed cats loved to gossip. Felines were never privy to family discussions and were kept out of the rooms where family talks occurred.

Better than Catching the Bouquet

When a cat is grooming her whiskers in front of a group of people, the first human the cat lays her eyes on will be the next to be wed.

Walk Softly and Carry an Umbrella

In England, people believed that when a cat washed behind its ears, it was a sign that rain was on the way.

Ants in their Pants

A fidgety cat moving about restlessly foretold of strong winds approaching.

Mittens for Kittens

Cold weather is on the way when a cat sleeps with all paws tucked in under its body.

Overnight Nonsense

A cat spending the night outside making a loud racket supposedly warned of several days of bad weather on its way.

Sweet Dreams

If you dreamed of a tortoiseshell cat, you would have luck in matters of the heart. Dreaming of ginger cats foretold success in money and business. A nocturnal vision of a tabby ensured good fortune with your home, and multicolored cats represented luck in friendship. Being scratched by a cat in a dream predicted sickness or trouble.

Navigational Cats

The French once believed that a black cat could help find buried treasure. They would find an intersection where five roads met, then let the cat loose and let it lead them to their fortune.

Recipe for Fertility

The Pennsylvania Dutch believed that a cat placed in an empty cradle would grant a newlywed couple a home filled with children. In Scandinavian countries, cats represented fertility, while Hindus equated cats with childbirth.

Ahoy Kitty

Sailors believed that cats had the power to start a storm with the magic in their tails, so they fed them regularly to keep them content.

If the ship's cat was in front of a sailor as he headed to the pier, good luck would ensue, but if the cat crossed the sailor's path, bad luck was on the way.

If the cat approached a sailor on board, the man would have good fortune, but if the cat decided to stop halfway, the poor sailor was doomed.

The worst possible luck would befall the crew if they tossed a cat overboard.

If a sailor observed a cat licking its fur in the opposite direction, a hailstorm was brewing. But if the cat sneezed, only rain would come.

A good sailor's wife or fisherman's wife would be sure to have a black cat and keep it at home to prevent any misadventure for her mate at sea.

You wouldn't hear a loudly mewing cat on a ship because that was thought to mean a rough voyage lay ahead.

Looking for Love

A single woman wanting a marriage proposal would place three cat hairs under her pillow, and a dream would foretell who her true love would be.

If a proposal was offered but the maiden was undecided, she would wrap three cat hairs in paper and place them under the front steps overnight. The shape of a "y" for yes or "n" for no would appear when the paper was unwrapped.

Friendship Buster

Tea drinkers would look at the bottom of the cup for signs of their future. If the shape of a cat appeared, it meant that a friend wasn't loyal.

A Terrible Fate

Kicking a cat causes rheumatism in the leg you used.

Farmers guilty of killing a cat will suffer mysterious cattle losses.

Drowning a cat condemns you to the same fate.

A cat has nine lives. For three he plays, for three he strays and for the last three he stays.

–American and English proverb

Death

If mourners saw a black cat sitting on a newly dug grave, it indicated that the devil had taken that soul.

Two cats engaging in combat on top of a grave meant they were fighting over the departed one's soul.

When a man witnesses two cats fighting, his death is just around the corner.

During a funeral procession, if a black cat was seen, another family member would die soon.

Scottish immigrants believed if they touched a cat that had entered a parlor containing a dead body, they would go blind.

In Transylvania, people believed a corpse would turn into a vampire if a cat jumped over it.

Like Winning the Lottery

When encountering a one-eyed cat, make sure you spit on your thumb and use it to stamp the middle of your palm while making a wish. The wish will come true.

Healing with Feces
During the time of ancient Romans, healers used cat feces to concoct medicines for a variety of ailments. A recipe for treating wounds and burns included cat dung, honey, spices and fat. Obviously hydrogen peroxide had not been invented yet.

An early treatment for baldness was an ointment containing cat excrement. Ironically, the same salve was used to remove body hair.

To Soup or Not to Soup
A broth made from boiling a black cat was thought by American colonists to cure tuberculosis, but no one wanted to take the chance of being cursed for killing a feline.

It's Not Your Grandmother's Chicken Soup
Anyone suffering from dizziness, fever or seizures during the
Middle Ages was given a remedy containing cat poop and wine.

A Little Tail

Rubbing the tail of a black cat on an eye afflicted with a sty was
thought to be a cure for the ailment.

Zapped by Angels

Scottish folk believed that bolts of lightning were sent by angels to
rid cats of evil spirits. When storms came, cats were sent outside.

No-see-ums

The Arabs held the secret to the magician's disappearing act.
They believed that if you wore a cats-eye stone, you would
become invisible.

Color Me Rich, Lucky and Safe

An ancient Buddhist superstition linked the color of a cat to personal wealth. A white feline indicated the home would always be filled with silver, while a dark cat ensured a house would have perpetual gold.

The Irish and Scottish cat owners preferred tortoiseshell cats because they supposedly brought good luck.

A superstition of unknown origin had people believing that a cat with a tricolored coat would protect them from fire.

Cat Magic

Cat magic was practiced by small groups of people from different cultures. Practitioners would perform rituals to entice a variety of outcomes with cats as their co-partners. Naturally, discarded whiskers or hair from a cat were used to perform magic that might bring prosperity, healing, a new love or children. Some spells included other items such as candles and thread and were combined with chants during certain phases of the moon to promote healing. The practice went underground for several centuries when cats were being persecuted. Cat magic is once again practiced in some countries in Europe and in the U.S.

Lucky Ornament

Maneki Neko, or "beckoning cat," is the most common good luck charm found throughout Japan. The ceramic figure sits on its haunches with one paw raised. The figure rose to fame during the latter part of the Edo period (1603–1867), replacing phallic symbols that normally adorned shelves in homes and businesses.

Lucky Colors

The most popular *Maneki Neko* is tricolored, perhaps because the gene responsible for tricolored male cats is rare. Other popular versions include white—representing purity—and black. Black cats are considered lucky in Japan and are believed to have the ability to chase away demons and cure illness in children. A current popular belief about black *Maneki Neko* among Japanese women is that they keep stalkers at bay. The rare red beckoning cats also provide insurance against evil spirits and illness. A gold-colored figure attracts money, while a pink one brings love.

Dressed up Luck
Maneki Neko come in a variety of colors and most sport a red collar with a bell, while some can be found wearing an apron. Other garments or attachments can include bibs, hats or gold coins.

Which High Five?
More than half of the talismans have a raised paw, beckoning clients to enter a retail outlet. A raised right paw is for attracting money and good fortune. The height of the paw also has significance. The higher the reach, the better the access to the cat's lucky magic.

The Birth of an Idol

Four legends remain about the origin of *Maneki Neko*.

Lord Li Naotaka was a poor monk living at a financially challenged temple near Kyoto in the 17th century. Despite his impoverishment, he shared his meager allotment of food with his cat.

During a rainstorm on his way home from hunting, Naotaka took refuge under a tree. He spied a cat beckoning him towards the temple compound. Curiously, while he ventured towards the unknown cat, lightning struck the tree. As a result, the lord became the temple patron, and afterwards, money was no longer scarce.

The temple was renamed Goutokuji, and the walls featured paintings of bobtail cats. When the cat that had prompted Naotaka away from the tree died, it was buried in the temple's cat cemetery and the *Maneki Neko* was created to honor the mystical cat.

Today, the temple houses many beckoning cat statues, and owners of missing or ill cats attend the temple to leave prayers for their animals on prayer boards.

Not So Lucky

A courtesan by the name of Usugumo living in Tokyo during the Edo period had a cat as her constant companion. Usugumo was about to leave her room when her cat grasped the hem of her kimono and would not let go. The building's landlord came to help remove the feline, who by now was more than insistent that the courtesan remain in the room.

Thinking the animal was evil, the landlord beheaded the cat with his sword. The head flew towards the ceiling, destroying a snake that was poised to kill the courtesan.

Usugumo was filled with sadness and guilt over the wrongful death of her cat. A client of the courtesan bought a carved statue of a cat to bring her joy. The image later became known as *Maneki Neko*.

Listen to Your Cat

A destitute woman living in Tokyo was forced to abandon her pet cat. A short time later, while sleeping, she dreamed of her cat. The feline told the woman to create a clay statue resembling its likeness. Compelled to follow the directions of the dream, the woman created the statues and soon began selling the cat idols she created, bringing her good fortune.

Shop Till You Drop

One final theory on the origin of the lucky cat is a simple tale of two similar shops next door to one another. One day, one of the shop owners placed a cat statue in his front display window. Business flourished, so his neighboring competitor also put a cat statue in the window.

GEORGIE

She came as part of a package deal. A rural coworker of mine was moving back to the city and needed a home for her country-loving dog and cat—but I had to take them both. Not wanting to separate two buddies, I agreed to the proposal and adopted Georgie, a calico feline with striking moon yellow eyes, and her sidekick Kip, a border collie cross.

Georgie was fiercely independent and wanted no part of long human cuddles when a casual pat on the head would do. Okay, I thought, at least she won't be crowding my feet at mealtime or ambushing me for attention. Other than Kip, Georgie preferred her own company and ignored the dozen other cats and kittens residing with me. A low growl would slip out if the other felines moved anywhere near her comfort zone. And soon all came to accept her loner, "I'm better than you" personality.

A short time after acquiring Georgie, my family planned to move to another acreage about nine miles away. With a manufactured home, part of the relocation would be smooth, but transporting animals—reluctant car passengers at best—would be trickier. The crisp November morning showed promise of a glitch-free moving day, and the only task I had before heading to work was transporting the cats to their new home.

I herded the cats into their shed and carefully loaded them two at a time into my car. A head count revealed Georgie had some-how slipped out unnoticed, and she wouldn't respond to my frantic calls. My search yielded nothing and the furry crew in the car was getting antsy as they crawled and snaked their way underneath the seats, anxious to find an exit.

Feeling guilty as I drove to my new acreage, I tried to bolster myself by thinking Georgie would hang around the old home site, and I could pick her up after work. Driving a car brimming with cats kept my mind and eyes occupied as I hugged the mid-dle of the gravel road, hoping not to have an accident with an anx-ious group of animals that all wanted a turn at driving.

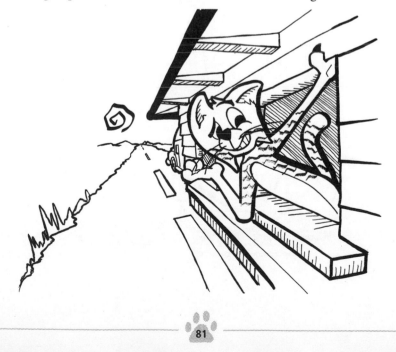

The movers arrived and lifted the manufactured home onto the truck, while I, after dropping off my feline posse, spent the day at work wondering about Georgie.

After work, I arrived at the new site to see that our home was intact. I was stunned to see Georgie meandering about her new digs. I assumed my husband had found her and had given her a lift in his truck. He could not take the credit for transporting Georgie; instead, he revealed how clever the feline had been.

Georgie had hitched a ride on the trailer that carried the manufactured home. When the movers began to unload and level the structure at the new site, out popped Georgie from underneath the house. It took everyone by surprise, except for Georgie.

She walked around her new hunting grounds like it was no big deal to make her own travel arrangements. Besides, it would have been beneath her to travel with the commoners during the morning cat taxi service.

ROCK-O

Rock-o, our neutered Snowshoe, is an inquisitive fellow that has developed some unique behavior traits and fetishes.

Rock-o loves to be in the bathroom when I am taking a shower, for which he received the nickname "Peeping Tom."

But it was his fondness for female apparel that had the household in a laughing fit.

While we were watching TV late one night, we heard Rock-o make an unusual sound as he approached, and everyone's head turned to witness him carrying a bra into the living room. The nosy thief had dug the piece of apparel out of the laundry basket. We now have laundry collectors with lids.

There is no more intrepid explorer than a kitten.

–Jules Champfleury

SHORTBOX

Something white darted into my peripheral vision as I arrived home on a mellow October evening. The blip resembled a miniature rabbit, which I thought was impossible given the time of year. Once inside the house I didn't give it a second thought until I caught the grin on my husband's face.

"Did you happen to see anything?" he casually asked.

"Why, yes I did," was my reply as I explained the flash of fur-covered lightning.

Earlier in the day, a neighbor had discovered a six- to eight-week-old kitten in a culvert, and a search for the owner commenced. No one from the nearby acreages was missing a kitten, and it was too young to have traveled much farther. My husband agreed to bring him home to join the rest of our motley crew.

Curious about the mysterious orphan, I went to investigate the newcomer, but the skittish kitten wanted no part of getting caught. With a can of wet cat food in one hand and a wagging arm to keep the other mooches away, I stilled failed to nab him. In ambush and stealth mode, I hung over the deck on my belly and scooped him up.

Frightened but relieved, the tom kitten settled enough for me to examine him. His front legs were abnormally short. Gray ears, a tabby-striped, dark tail and three splashes of ecru on his white fur gave him a unique look, and I counted six toes on one paw. It was his peculiar structure that sent me searching through my cat research for answers.

The unnamed feline resembled a munchkin and was built like a low-rider. It was amazing that we'd found each other considering the risks that face a lone kitten in the country.

He now has a name—Shortbox—and he is fearless when it comes to the other larger, outdoor males. The ladies like him, too.

Shortbox comes in daily for playtime with our indoor cat, Rock-o, and Rock-o's half brother Dieter. The trio runs amok with cat toys while providing us with hours of entertainment as three different age and weight classes mix it up in the living room. Shortbox excels at speed and agility against the larger and older pair. As we continue to watch how he matures and reveals his personality, Shortbox adds a new dimension to our cat ranch.

One reason we admire cats is for their proficiency in one-upmanship. They always seem to come out on top, no matter what they are doing, or pretend they do.

–Barbara Webster

TOP THIS

Dogs have owners; cats have staff.

–Unknown

Who Packed the Parachute?
Andy is the free-fall champion of Florida, pre-1981. The pet of former state Senator Ken Myer fell 16 stories from a Miami high-rise and put cliff divers to shame.

Tubby Tabby

Himmy, an Australian tabby, was deemed the heaviest cat in the world. The feline from Down Under weighed in at a whopping 47 pounds. *The Guinness Book of Records* no longer recognizes this category so as not to encourage owners to take their cats to an all-you-can-eat buffet daily.

Longest Cat
Leo, a Maine Coon living with Frieda Ireland and Carroll Damron in Chicago, is a large fellow. He measures 48 inches from nose tip to the end of his tail. This blue-cheese–loving, mammoth-sized feline has paws large enough to fit in a child's size two shoes.

Either the Cake is too Small, or There Are too Many Candles
Cream Puff had a lot of life and stamina to hang around planet Earth for 38 years and 3 days. The Austin, Texas, owner also owned the previous old-timer record holder—Granpa Rexs Allen, a sphynx who lived to the age of 34 years, 2 months.

A Lot of Cat Begatting
This record has held for more than 50 years. Dusty, a prolific tabby, gave birth to 420 kittens in her childbearing years. Her last delivery was a solo kitten in June 1952.

Itty-Bitty Kitty

An apt name for the record holder of the smallest-ever cat, Tinker Toy was a male blue-point Himalayan. The pet of Katrina and Scott of Illinois measures 2.5 inches tall and 7.5 inches long. He passed away in 1997.

The current living record holder is also an American cat, Itse Bitse. The Himalayan Siamese cross, owned by Mayo and Dee Whitton, is 3.75 inches tall and measures 15 inches from nose to tail.

Air Miles

Humphrey could have collected quite a few points; instead, he received notoriety as the most traveled feline. The cat flew 600,000 miles after escaping from his carrier inside a Canadian commercial aircraft.

Longest Whiskers

Well, it's not quite a handlebar mustache, but Missi's whiskers did get her into the *2007 Guinness Book of Records*. The Maine coon, owned by Kaija Killonen of Finland, has tactile hairs that measure 7.5 inches long.

Big Brood

A four-year-old Burmese by the name of Tarawood Antigone holds the record for largest litter. She gave birth to 19 kittens in August 1970, but only 15 survived. A close second goes to a Persian named Bluebell. She had 14 kittens, and they all survived.

Largest Litter
The record is still intact from August 17, 1992, when one very pregnant female gave birth to 19 kittens.

Old Mama

A maternal cat by the name of Kitty had her last batch of kittens at the ripe old age of 30.

Say What?

A Japanese company has built a device that will translate what your cat is mewing about. About the size of a Blackberry, the translator, when placed next to a "talking" cat, interprets it's sounds and displays the words on a screen. Meowlingual, created by the Takeda company, costs under $100 and will eventually be available in an English version.

WORKING CATS

Army Cats

Cats lived in the trenches with soldiers during World War I doing what they do best—rodent control.

Passing Gas

In 1535, artillery officer Christopher of Hapsburg wrote about using cats to dispense poisonous gas to the enemy. The European soldier explained that bottles of poisonous fumes were attached to cats, with the opening facing the tail. The furry combatants were then sent out towards the opposing troops, their bottles spewing the deadly gas around the enemy.

Early Warning System

The British drafted cats for duty during World War I. To detect the possible use of chemical gas by the German enemy, 500 felines were dispatched to the front-line trenches. Like the proverbial canary in the mineshaft, these courageous warriors would sense a chemical attack, and their unfortunate reaction served as a warning to the human soldiers. No record exists indicating whether the cat troops returned home to England after the war.

Usher Cat

For two decades, Beerbohm was the resident exterminator for London's Globe Theatre. The large tabby, born in the mid-1970s, often amused the audience with cameo appearances onstage, much to the chagrin of the actors. A brush with death earned him a special spot in the lobby of the theater, where his portrait was placed. Beerbohm spent his golden years with the theater's carpenter. The feline passed away in 1995.

Bomb Brigade

Many peopled were spared from disaster thanks to the heightened awareness of cats. Pet cats in Britain during World War II could differentiate the sound of friendly aircraft from those of the enemy. Before the sky would rain bombs, cats were observed to take shelter, warning humans of the impending blitz.

Medal for Mettle

The Dickin Medal, an animal equivalent of the Victoria Cross for heroism, was awarded to only one cat among 60 recipients.

Discovered in a Hong Kong dockyard and smuggled aboard the HMS *Amethyst* by a British seaman, Simon, a black and white moggy, was soon employed catching rats aboard the frigate.

In April 1949, while heading up the Yangtze River in China for guard duty, the ship came under fire from communist Chinese forces. The vessel sustained numerous hits, and the crew had many casualties and fatalities. Besides the salvo damage, the ship also ran aground.

Not giving up the fight, the *Amethyst* finally limped to freedom after being trapped by the Chinese on the river for 101 days.

Simon was injured in the ordeal but soon returned to active duty while maintaining the crew's moral. For his bravery and service, Simon was chosen to receive the highest honor. Unfortunately, he passed away from a virus less than two weeks before the award presentation, and the Dickin was awarded posthumously.

Cat TV

Movies about cats, movies with cats...how about movies for cats?
The plot is nonexistent, but the feline audience won't mind;
viewing birds, running squirrels and bouncing balls will be a bit
more edgy than a nighttime drama.

The American cat-food company behind the video found that
almost one-quarter of pet owners change the channel to a TV
program that they believe their animals enjoy.

How's Your Two-Step?

Growing in popularity with classes, books and clubs sprouting up
annually, cat dancing was actually mentioned in a 17th-century
nursery rhyme:

Hey diddle diddle,
The cat and the fiddle,
The cow jumped over the moon.

The earlier version of this whimsical set of words was linked to
a witch's chant. It used the term
"heigh, diddle, daddle," which at
the time meant "come and shake"
or was an invitation to dance.
Puritans frowned on cat
dancing, believing it to
be the work of the devil
and pushed the practice
underground.

The art of dancing with
cats made a comeback in
the '70s and is flourishing
throughout the world.
However, when people learn to dance
with felines, they use stuffed animals to practice their moves.

Astrocat

Felix was nicknamed the "Astrocat" after completing a successful mission away from Earth. The former USSR space program used a variety of animals as subjects for space travel, and in 1963, it was the luck of the draw for felines. The Russians rounded up more than a dozen cats to begin a rigorous training program that included compression and centrifuge chambers.

On October 1, 1963, Felix climbed aboard a capsule attached to a French rocket and was catapulted 130 miles above the Earth from the Algerian desert. Instead of orbiting the planet, the space vessels separated and Felix descended to terra firma. The feline astronaut and capsule were safely retrieved.

Felix's journey was commemorated on a stamp three decades after his courageous voyage.

A Hair of the Cat

One of the oldest operational Scotch-whiskey distilleries in Scotland, Glenturret employed a cat named Towser to control the resident rodent population. The longhaired tortoiseshell made the *Guinness Book of Records* for being such a prolific mouser in her almost 24-year career. Mice in Scotland would quiver when they heard the name Towser; she is reported to have single-handedly killed 28,899 mice. When Towser died in 1987, a cat by the name of Amber replaced her but didn't live up to her predecessor's reputation. Amber kept her job despite her poor work performance, but when she died, the search was on for a new candidate.

The advertisement might have read "Wanted: One cat with extraordinary hunting skills that can work unsupervised and has good public relations." A cat psychologist was even consulted during the search. Nine applicants were short listed from a few of Scotland's animal shelters, but staff couldn't decide between two finalists.

A decision was made to keep them both, and the seven that were not chosen found good homes as a result of the publicity. The exploits of Towser and her work ethic were recognized with a bronze statue located at the visitor site at Glenturret.

Going Postal

Cats were working for the British mail service as early as 1868. In their official status, they protected packages, which often contained perishable food, from certain destruction by free-roaming rodents. The Controller of London's Money Order Office allotted a weekly stipend for each efficient mouser employed at museums and similar establishments. Over one century's worth of correspondence between the post office and the Controller, about regular cat care cost increases, was preserved and published in a book.

Pulitzer Pussycats

Ancient Egyptians staffed cats in their libraries, the Russians employed cats in museums and libraries for more than two centuries, and today, roughly 700 cats call libraries around the world their home.

An American woman, Phyllis Lahti, created the Library Cat society in 1987. The organization was created after Phyllis administered care to a homeless cat during a bitter winter storm and took him to her place of employment—the library—to reside.

Titled Cats

At the Maritime Museum of the Atlantic, located in Halifax, Nova Scotia, employed felines are referred to as Rodent Control Officers (RCOs). Over the years, a few RCOs have been a threat to the rat population, but it was Erik that caused a stir when he disappeared.

He was a scruffy kitten when he came to the attention of museum employees in the summer of 2000. Unable to locate the animal's owner, the staff gave Erik a collar and the title of RCO. Less than two months after his arrival, Erik vanished, and the term "catnapped" was tossed around. The wandering youngster found himself downtown without his identifying collar, begging for food, and a government employee couldn't say no. She scooped the little fellow up and took him home after work.

Within a few days, the revelation that Erik was the missing RCO prompted a reunification. Erik was back on duty 10 days after being AWOL.

At the Bottom of the World

Ginge resided at the British Antarctic Survey on Signy Island in 1963. His sole responsibility was staff entertainment and morale boosting at the isolated station. The friendly feline was known to go outdoors, practicing his hunting skills on the native birds.

It was Ginge's high kill count that brought him under the scrutiny of the station's chief biologist. The verdict was that Ginge had to go. Fortunately, the cat was spared a mercy killing when a staff member required medical treatment, and passage to civilization was arranged for the pair.

A home was found for Ginge in the UK, but life back at the British Antarctic Survey was never quite the same without the companionship of the polar cat.

Northern Cats

You couldn't be a wimp and work in commercial refrigeration plants in Pittsburgh during the 19th century, so a breed was developed to withstand the frigid temperatures during lengthy rodent patrols.

Rats were pervasive and caused costly damage to stored foods; only a super cat similar to winter-hardy Canadian wild cats could eliminate the problem. Successful breeding produced a hunter, with a thick body parka, that sabotaged any plans the rats had to take over the world.

 Although most castles in Britain are no longer residences and instead have been turned into tourist attractions, many still employ cats to control the rodent population.

Moscow Cats Theatre

This troupe of working and entertaining felines has humans pinching themselves in disbelief. Trained cats perform an array of circus-style acts among other incredible feats in mini-plays.

The man behind Moscow Cats Theater, Yuri Kuklachev has assembled and trained an amazing cast of furry characters—120 at last count—that delight audiences worldwide with unique circus theater performances. Kuklachev revealed the secret of his success: "It's not me who trains cats; it's cats who train me, and I just watch them."

And to think, Moscow Cats Theatre began with a stray kitten Kuklachev found in 1971.

Working Convent Cats

A cat has a good work ethic...when it wants to. Which is why, in Cypress, they were pressed into action to destroy large numbers of snakes in the fourth century.

Years of drought had reduced the human population while increasing the infestation of deadly serpents. Armies of elite cats were brought to the island from Egypt to fight the snake war while being housed and cared for at a monastery known as St. Nicholas. Today, the convent is known as St. Nicholas of the Cats and is inhabited by five nuns and roughly 200 cats.

Many nursing homes caring for the elderly regularly invite felines to visit their clients. The effect is profound for both animals and humans, providing positive experiences that have therapeutic benefit.

Barn Buddies

Some racehorse breeders press cats into service to steady the nerves of their high-strung champions. Felines seem to have a calming effect on horses and can become very dedicated to their equine friends.

The Godolphin Arabian, a well-known stallion in the 18th century, had a companion cat. Upon the horse's death in 1753, the feline could not be budged from the corpse and remained with the horse until it was buried. The cat then quietly disappeared and was later found dead in the hayloft.

Concierge or Mascot?

Manhattan's Algonquin Hotel has had a lot of famous guests, but it will be remembered more for the resident cats it employs. Rusty, a tortie tom, lived at the hotel during the late 1920s and '30s, when it was frequented by the likes of James Thurber, Dorothy Parker and Alexander Woolcott. His job was to keep the vermin at bay. Next came Hamlet, also a mouser and mascot. Matilda, a stray kitten, took Hamlet's place.

Musical Mews

The cat organ, used to honor Philip II in 1549 as he paraded through the streets of Brussels, was more of a twisted, cruel amusement for humans than a feline profession. A box was designed that held up to 20 cats firmly captive, separated by partitions. Their tails were individually attached to the keyboard with string so that each time a key was pressed, a tail was pulled, producing a vocal reaction from the cat.

Cat Laws

If cats during the reign of Hywel Dda, Prince of Wales, could have recommended sainthood, they would have given it to this medieval ruler for decreeing cat protection laws.

Howel the Good, as he is known today, saw magnificent worth in felines as pest assassins. Believing that they deserved more respect among humans, the Welsh monarch assigned a dollar figure to cats and kittens and initiated penalties for those found guilty of killing or stealing a cat.

A feline's worth was dependent on its hunting skills, its ability to reproduce and who its owner was. Compensation in some cases was grain. To determine how much of the cereal seed was to be forfeited as a penalty for the crime, the cat's corpse was hung by the tail and grain was piled up until it reached the same height as the tip of the cat's tail.

AGE

Happy Birthday

If you are celebrating you kitty's birthday and his tuna fish cupcake has only one candle, he is the equivalent of being a teenager in human years.

The following chart converts a cat's age:

Cat years	Human years
1 month	5–6 months
2 months	9–10 months
3 months	2–3 years
4 months	5–6 years
5 months	8–9 years
6 months	10 years
8 months	13 years
1 year	15 years
2 years	24 years
3 years	28 years
4 years	32 years
5 years	36 years
6 years	40 years
7 years	44 years
8 years	48 years
9 years	52 years
10 years	56 years
11 years	60 years
12 years	64 years
15 years	76 years
18 years	88 years
21 years	100 years

The chart represents a rule of thumb approach to determining a cat's age and its stage in life compared to humans. Development from a newborn kitten to an adult cat is compressed into roughly two years, unlike humans, who need many years to reach adulthood. After a cat reaches maturity, the ratio levels out and four cat years pass for every human year.

A CAT BY ANY OTHER NAME

How do you say "cat" in Spanish? Why *gato,* of course.
In France, the word is *chat.*
In Poland, you would say *kot.*
The Japanese call out *neko.*
In Germany, owners say *katze.*
Ancient Egyptians used the word *miu*; the modern term in that country is *mau.*
In Hebrew, a cat is known as *chatul.*
The Chinese say *mao.*
In Swahili, you would say *paka.*
England's nickname for cat is "moggy."
In Sweden and Norway, they say *katt.*
Italians call out *gatto.*
Icelanders say *kattur.*
A Greek cat is called *gata.*
A Turkish feline is known as *kedi.*
Hungarian cats come to *macska.*
Billy is the word used to call a cat in India.
In Arabic, *biss* is for a male cat and *bissie* is for a female.
The Dutch say *poes.*
Malayans can be heard saying *kuching.*
The Mohawk term is *tako's.*
While in Indonesia, you will hear *kutjing.*
The Welsh have three terms of endearment: *cath, kath* or *cetti.*
A Russian male cat is known as *kot,* and a female is called *koshka.*
A Maltese cat comes to *qattus.*
Hawaiians use one of two words to get a cat's attention: *owan* and *popoki.*
A Finnish cat is known as *kissa.*
Lithuanians say *kate.*

KITTY MISCELLANY

Contraception

Non-surgical birth control for cats is widely practiced in Israel. Just like the human version, a hormone-laced pill tricks the female cat's body into thinking it is pregnant. Not every cat is a cooperative recipient of the oral contraceptives, but it is still an effective method of controlling the feline population and is said to prevent the birth of 20,000 kittens per year.

Sterilization law

Rhode Island became the first place in the U.S. to pass a mandatory spay/neuter law for cats. Governor Don Carcieri signed the proactive birth control legislation to reduce the increasing number of cats euthanized at state shelters.

Paint Me Expensive

Pablo Picasso turned the art world upside down with his unique style of expression on canvas and in other media. But it was a 1941 portrait of his mistress and a cat that made headlines for its selling price.

The painting, "Dora Maar au Chat," depicts Picasso's lover poised regally on a chair with a black cat standing behind her. Critics and historians say Picasso compared the personality of his mistress to that of a cat—lending extra significance to the portrait.

The artwork sold for $95 million at Sotheby's Auction House.

In a cat's eye, all things belong to cats.
–English proverb

Inmates Running the Asylum

For the past 20 years, Bob Walker and Frances Mooney have continually spent time and money renovating their southern California house to suit the needs of their cats.

"One-hundred-and-forty feet of elevated walkway have been constructed to allow our felines to pass through walls and frolic overhead," said one of the homeowners.

To view the world's largest kitty jungle gym, log on to www.thecathouse.com.

Who Needs Who?

Mounting evidence suggests that humans need pets. Some of the research cites the following reasons:

- Cats can help combat loneliness. They make great company and owners have been known to talk to them.
- Separation from adult children or other family members and farm animals or nature can cause anxiety for some people; however, having a pet such as a cat often alleviates or reduces those feelings.
- Purpose and productivity are by-products of owning a cat. For people who live alone, having a cat provides a purpose because owners must adhere to the routine of feeding and grooming the animal and changing the litter box.
- Protection might seem like a farfetched advantage to having a cat, but some cats have saved their owners from fires and some cat owners don't feel as vulnerable while home alone.
- For those suffering from hypertension, petting a cat can help to lower blood pressure.
- Cats keep you out of the doctor's office. Statistics show that individuals with pets make fewer trips to the doctor, especially for non-serious medical issues.
- Depression is kept at bay for pet owners.
- Companionship between humans and cats promotes a bond that helps people endure troubling times. Cats can also help take the edge off stressful experiences for seniors.

Looking for Love

Cat owners can search for a relationship with another cat owner online. There are several online pet-dating services in the U.S. that offer a matchmaking service for cat owners. Whether you are a talkative Siamese or a high-maintenance Persian, there's a possible match made in cyberspace just waiting for you.

Big and Small
Some of the bigger breeds can tip the scales up around 22 pounds. Maine coons range from 7 to 22 pounds, while rag-dolls, Norwegian forest and Siberian cats weigh in at between 10 and 20 pounds and Turkish Vans hold steady between 7 and 19 pounds.

Small in Stature, Big in Heart
Singapuras are the smallest breed, with females weighing as little as 4 pounds and males almost twice that, at 7 pounds. Other lightweights include the Cornish rex, Devon rex and Japanese bobtail, all ranging between 6 and 9 pounds.

A Feline Mardi Gras
In Belgium, modern cat worship takes the form of a May festival every three years. Its beginnings were cruel, but the festival has evolved to become a massive celebration of, what else, cats.

Centuries ago, when cats were persecuted, once a year felines were rounded up and dropped off a towering building without a parachute. If any victims survived, it was a good omen—a good harvest would come.

The cruelty existed until 1817, and the festival was resurrected in Yprés twice in the 1930s and then again after World War II, but this time, cat mannequins were substituted for the toss. The Festival of Cats or *Kattestoet,* as it is known in Belgium, grew enormously popular over the years, and because of the tremendous amount of planning that was required for the event, it became necessary to cut it down to once every three years instead of holding the festival annually. Other activities include a three-hour parade paying homage to feline history, a "Witches Brew" and a fireworks display. It continues to be a festival that locals and visitors alike look forward to attending.

Higher Education

Some vet clinics offer kitten classes, though they are more for the benefit of the humans than the kittens. The schooling offers an opportunity to learn about normal cat behavior and develop skills for training the kitten at home. Kittenhood is a critical time for your pet to learn socialization skills, not only with humans, but also with other felines.

Me-ality TV

I wish I could have been a fly on the wall when the promotions department came up with the idea of a reality show using cats. The Meow Mix cat food company rounded up 10 homeless cat contestants from different areas in the U.S. The felines were housed for 10 days under the watchful eye of the camera while the public could vote for who stayed and who went. On the company's website, Ellis was declared the viewers' choice winner. She will get the position of VP of Research and Development for the company, while the other nine cats found permanent homes.

NOTEWORTHY CATS

9/11 Survivors

The term "miracle" gets used a lot, yet it is an apt description of the following story:

During the recovery process of 9/11 after the World Trade Center collapsed, rescuers made an unusual discovery. In a basement area, among debris and rubble, a cat was curled up in a box of napkins. Upon closer inspection, three kittens were discovered inside the box as well. The remarkable survivors received a clean bill of health and were renamed Flag, Hope, Freedom and Amber.

Cat on a Fast Tin Roof

Have you ever had one of those days when you should have just stayed in bed? That was probably what one Idaho motorist was thinking when she found her cat had hitched a ride on the roof of her car.

Torri Hutchinson was cruising down the Interstate when a passing motorist kept pointing to her vehicle and trying to get her attention. Relenting, the female driver pulled over but cautiously kept her doors locked and the engine running. The unidentified male driver excitedly ran up to her car while shouting, "Your cat! Your cat!"

Looking around inside her car, Hutchinson could not see her cat. While she searched her car, the Good Samaritan removed the orange tabby from the roof of the stationary vehicle. It seems the daredevil had climbed outside the vehicle through an open window when Hutchinson stopped for gas. The feline car surfed for 10 miles before it was rescued.

Bear Beware

There is one cat in New Jersey that even a bear didn't want to mess with.

Jack, a 10-year-old orange and white tabby, took exception to an interloper in a neighbor's backyard. The clawless feline hustled the trespassing bear up a tree with a barrage of hissing and kept it hostage with a penetrating stare and vocal harassment. After about 10 minutes, the bruin gingerly eased down the tree and made its escape. Jack chased the bear into the bushes but ended the pursuit when he was called home.

Cat Headstone

A tombstone marking the burial site of a cat in England turned out to be a rare artifact. A stonemason found the limestone image of St. Peter at a quarry and used it as a gravestone for Winkle when the tabby passed away. It was an amateur historian that spied the 10th-century carving. The medieval relief fetched close to $500,000 at Sotheby's auction house.

Better than a High School Reunion
Only Sneakers can tell the tale of his 10-year journey, and he isn't talking.

The black, longhaired feline went missing from Seattle, Washington, in 1996. Flyers and newspaper ads described the missing cat, and the cat's family went door to door, pleading for the public's assistance. Sneakers was never found

Fast-forward to June 2006, when a black, longhaired cat was brought to an animal shelter in Sacramento, California. The kitty's microchip revealed a number that was traced back to Seattle. Allison MacEwan was probably flooded with elation and disbelief when she learned Sneakers had been found.

Accidental Arsonist

Unbelievably, a dog once died trying to rescue a cat from a house fire.

A disabled Wisconsin woman lost both best friends when her cat jumped onto a table, knocking over a burning candle, which started a blaze. Her 13-year-old dog was specially trained to be an assistant to his owner and demonstrated his skills during the emergency by retrieving the woman's artificial leg, which at the time was not attached to her body, and a phone so she could call for help. The woman was able to get out of the home while waiting for the firefighters. The German shepherd cross went back into the flame-filled home to rescue the cat but, sadly, both animals died in the fire.

A Smoke Alarm in Fur
An Australian family can thank their cat for his fast thinking. Timmy, the family's tabby, was anxiously trying to wake his owner by scratching his face. A fire had broken out in the home, and Timmy was insistent that his owner do something about it. The tabby's actions woke the owner and a call to the fire department brought help. Because of the quick actions of the cat, the home suffered only minor damage.

Cat Burglars

The term "cat burglar" is usually given to a human thief; however, a pair of English cats reclaimed the title.

It all started when Major Benjie, an Oriental tabby, entered a neighbor's house through the cat door and returned home with a toy. A copy-cat crime occurred when Major Benjie's roommate, Georgie, followed suit but brought home an expensive watch. The pair was busted and received house arrest, where they now spend their days as peeping toms.

Cat Buried Alive

Mr. Whiskers of Calgary, Alberta, is considered to be a miracle cat after surviving two weeks as an accidental hostage beneath a set of outdoor stairs in 2002.

The five-year-old, tricolored tabby wandered beneath a neighbor's concrete steps and remained trapped when workers began leveling the yard, pushing the dirt to the stairs. Construction equipment in the new subdivision drowned out Mr. Whiskers' pleas for help for 12 days before the homeowners began hearing his voice. For the next three days, they cruised around the home searching out the source of the mewing. When workers removed the soil surrounding the steps, they found a fragile, but alive, cat.

Remarkably, Mr. Whiskers survived his ordeal by sucking moisture from the soil of his cramped quarters. His family nursed him back to health.

Crime Fighter

A Brooklyn kitten named Fred is heralded for helping to nab a fake veterinarian.

Fred, a stray, went undercover after police received a complaint about a shoddy operation performed on a Boston terrier. Police wired an apartment and recorded the bogus vet collecting cash to perform a neutering service on the kitten from an undercover officer acting as Fred's owner. After the man was busted for treating animals without a license, the Brooklyn District Attorney recognized Fred for his work.

Gotta Go

A Pennsylvania cat owner could have renamed her feline Houdini after a bizarre disappearing act.

In the summer of 1965, Barbara Paule was driving her van in Dayton, Ohio, accompanied by her pet cat, Muddy Water White. The brazen cat jumped out of the vehicle and vanished. Three years later, a cat showed up at Paule's Pennsylvania home, acting like it owned the place. It took three days of feeding the stray before Paule realized it was her escape artist, Muddy Water White. A veterinarian confirmed the identification of the cat, which had traveled a journey of at least 450 miles.

Katrina Survivor

In times of natural disaster, most energy is expended towards human rescue and the subsequent news coverage. With pets playing a larger role in the lives of their families, aid efforts during disasters are expanding at a rapid pace, as was witnessed in the aftermath of Katrina.

Mississippi resident Bill Harris endured three days on a chair, holding his cat and a two-way radio, to escape the rising waters. The good news is the 59-year-old was rescued and hospitalized. The bad news—Miss Kitty had to stay behind.

It was more than a week before Miss Kitty was finally located and captured by a Canadian volunteering assistance to Katrina survivors. The Good Samaritan drove the cat to Harris, where Miss Kitty leaped out of the arms of her rescuer and into the hospital bed of her "daddy."

Miss Kitty was credited with keeping Harris awake by mewing while waiting for help.

An "Inside" Story

For a Kansas family, "if these walls could talk" took on a whole new meaning.

Renovation plans for the Louisbourg home didn't include mewing walls, but that's what the owner and workers kept hearing, despite efforts to track the location of the unrelenting noise. It was the contractor who found the cat, which had been stuck under the enclosed bathtub for at least three weeks.

Once the cat was rescued and checked by a vet, the homeowners tried to locate its owners.

Mechanics 101

Owners of a Mazda MX5 spent three hours tearing it apart to rescue a cat.

The adventure started when Zoe Hartley and John Holmes took a drive to Blackpool, north of Liverpool, England. About 30 miles into their trip, they heard the desperate pleas of a cat. Stopping the car and searching in all of the usual places yielded nothing. Holmes took a gander under the vehicle and finally noticed the tomcat. Part of the undercarriage was dismantled to free the feline, who seemed unruffled by the harrowing trip. The vehicle owner had no association with the cat and assumed it was likely seeking a warm spot to snooze when it was taken on the trip from hell.

Parliamentary Cat

Humphrey, a handsome, black and white longhair, was roaming the streets of London a free cat one day, and the next day he was cozying up to British Prime Minister Margaret Thatcher.

When John Major took office, the moggy stayed behind, loyal to Number 10 Downing Street. He was fingered for killing four birds, then disappeared, with the media catching a whiff of a hot story.

Down the street, members at the Royal Army Medical College realized the cat they had adopted, fed and renamed was from the prime minister's residence. Humphrey was returned and reinstated as the First Mouser of the British Isles with complete media coverage.

Seasick and Homesick

In late November 2006, one cruise-bound feline shocked cargo workers when it shot out of a shipping container in England after a 17-day voyage from Israel.

Unloading a shipment in Whitworth, near the northwest coast of Britain, workers were startled when a white, four-legged stowaway bolted from the container after having traveled more than 2000 miles. The seafaring cat fled the scene and hid for several hours before being found by animal rescuers. The wary cat had to be coaxed out of hiding with a plate of tuna.

Suffering from many missed meals and dehydration, the wayward cat was in pretty good shape, said animal officers. While tracing the cat's owners, the cargo workers nicknamed the furry sailor Ziggy.

University Cat

It is a given that cats are intelligent, but one particular feline got an MBA.

A spammer offering university degrees online for cash was caught after Pennsylvanian authorities set up a sting operation using a cat as bait. An application for a bachelor's degree using a feline's name plus bogus education and work history was emailed to the scam artist.

The fake institution allegedly upped the designation because the applicant's employment history merited a higher degree. Within weeks, the official-looking document awarding the cat an MBA arrived. Officials took it one step further and requested the cat's transcript, which was sent, revealing a 3.5 GPA.

Shocking

After what Sparky went through, it's easy to see why some claim that cats have nine lives.

Wandering into an electric substation in Yorkshire, the tabby received an 11,000-volt shock. An onsite worker managed to pick the cat up while carefully avoiding a live wire transmitting 132,000 volts.

Sparky, as he was nicknamed, suffered burns to his paws, fur and whiskers, and was partially paralyzed from the incident. The cat's true owner saw a picture of Sparky and the story of the near-death event in the newspaper and was reunited with her pet, whose real name was Soxy.

Rescued Owner

Coffee, a two-year-old cat, was nominated for a bravery award in York, England, after saving its owner from a fire.

John Chislett was frying potatoes in a pan filled with oil and neglected to turn off the stove. While Chislett was napping, the pot of hot oil burst into flames, which began to spread. Coffee, alert to the situation, jumped on the owner and began biting his nose while butting up against the owner's head. The pair escaped the fire, and Coffee was treated for smoke inhalation.

Tandem Trouble

It was a flower show to remember for Mrs. Hardy, but not because of the beautiful foliage.

Hardy was packing up the lorry at her Hampshire home to participate in the annual Chelsea Flower Show in England. Unbeknownst to her, a pair of her four-month-old kittens had hitched a ride underneath the truck. The baby felines, perched a mere 2 feet above the pavement, clung to the undercarriage for three hours. The duo—Smoky and Dotty—was unharmed when Hardy discovered the wayward pair while unloading at the show.

Wall Cat Headlines

"The walls have ears" could be interpreted literally in a New York deli as rescuers tried numerous strategies to entice a kitten that had been trapped for 12 days behind a wall.

Eleven-month-old Molly kept the deli free of rodents and became wall-bound when she slipped into a slim opening between two buildings and dropped through a hole to the basement. Animal rescue tried bribing Molly with raw fish while they drilled an opening for a miniature camera to capture the drama and, perhaps, aid in retrieval. The activity frightened Molly, and she withdrew farther into the 19th-century structural maze. Molly's outcome is unknown.

Wheelchair Kitty

You won't find Speedy at the Indianapolis 500, but you will see a unique prosthetic aiding the biped cat to get around Millarsville, Pennsylvania.

As a kitten, Speedy was discovered living under a hedge with his siblings and stray mother. An elderly man clipping the bush noticed something terribly wrong with Speedy's back legs. A trip to the vet revealed the kitten had no pelvis. A plan was hatched to build a miniature mobile cart out of the kind of snap-together building kits used by children. Speedy adapted to his prototype wheelchair within a day and uses his front paws to power himself.

Seven More than the Owner

Tiger, the 27-toed kitty, has become Leduc, Alberta's, newest celebrity after completing her first U.S. tour with owner Garth Ukrainetz. The kitty had plenty of exposure thanks to Ukrainetz's promotion of her unusual, and supposedly lucky, overabundance of toes.

Some of the celebrity appearances made by the Leduc feline in the U.S. include the following:
- Fox 59 Indianapolis—Tiger made a live appearance on their breakfast show on June 13, 2001.
- The *Anderson Herald Bulletin*—Tiger made the front page on June 14, 2001.
- RTV6 (ABC) Indianapolis—A short documentary on Tiger aired on the evening news on June 18, 2001.
- WJZ13 (CBS) Baltimore—Tiger and Ukrainitz made an appearance on the WJZ morning show, the largest in the Baltimore–Washington, D.C., area on June 19, 2001. Tiger was a hit.
- *The Early Show* (CBS) New York City—Tiger got some brief exposure on CBS' nationally syndicated live morning show with weatherman/entertainment reporter Mark McEwan on June 22, 2001.

All in all Tiger was very well received down in the U.S. The kitty even loved the 100 hours of driving between Edmonton and New York City.

"Millions of Americans got to see her. The media was quite fascinated by her. Tiger was a great ambassador for Alberta," said Ukrainitz.

Tiger is one digit short of the record holder for the feline with the most toes.

Carbon Copy

Researchers in Texas picked the right moniker for the first cloned feline—CopyCat or "cc" for short. The kitten, born December 22, 2001, was the first cloned domestic pet. A year later, researchers noted that although cc has the same DNA as her mother, a calico named Rainbow, she doesn't look identical nor does she behave the same way.

Copy Cat was back in the news after giving birth to three healthy kittens (which were conceived the traditional way). Two of the kittens look like their grandmother Rainbow—or would cloning make her an aunt?—and the third baby resembles its father, a gray tabby.

Sweet

Without a forwarding address, Sugar managed to find the new home of his owners—1500 miles away.

The Woods were relocating to Oklahoma in 1951 and made arrangements for the neighbors to adopt Sugar. It seems the feline detested car rides, so a move was out of the question. Fourteen days after the Woods moved, Sugar disappeared from his new home with the neighbors.

More than a year had passed when Sugar leaped through the window of the Woods' new home right into the lap of Mrs. Woods. No one is certain how the cat managed to find his owners without knowledge of where they had moved to, but Sugar's identity was certain, based not only on the Persian's unique coloring but also on his malformed hip.

Fled the Scene
A Winnipeg, Manitoba, resident was observing a chase scene between a Husky dog and a cat, when the feline sought refuge in a tall tree, far above the aggressive canine. The witness tried for three days to persuade the feline, with food and idle conversation, to abandon his post. The cat wasn't buying it. The man

called around to find businesses outfitted with sky-reaching capabilities but had no success. The cat was finally rescued by a group of neighbors and then bolted from the Good Samaritans. From rescue victim to Olympic sprinter in the blink of an eye.

Tattoo Clue

Mitts, a Manitoba kitten, got a taste of the outside life and failed to return home. The owner made the usual inquiries any other owner would do when their pet goes missing. After a few months, hope faded that the animal would come home.

Three years after the kitten went missing, Sheri Talaga received an unexpected phone call—it wasn't a collect call from her cat but the next best thing. A cat had been brought to a humane society and staff traced the cat's tattoo back to Talaga.

The reunion was surreal for the relieved owner. Mitts had been well cared for during her absence but wouldn't reveal her home away from home.

Outlast, Outswim, Outsurvive

Oscar should earn the title of ultimate survivor not only for switching teams, but also for his miraculous rescues at sea.

The German mascot aboard the legendary *Bismarck* battleship escaped unharmed when the ship was attacked in 1941. Among the floating ship debris, Oscar was treading water for all he was worth. A British sailor rescued the dog-paddling cat and brought it aboard the Royal Navy destroyer HMS *Cossack*. The former German pet fell into a comfortable routine with his new British owners. Then the unthinkable happened. The *Cossack* went down five months after the *Bismarck,* and again Oscar was rescued from the grip of death on the Atlantic. The aircraft carrier *Ark Royal* took on Oscar, and again the vessel housing the feline came under fire by the enemy. A German U-boat torpedoed the *Ark Royal,* sending Oscar once more into the water.

He was rescued and retirement from the navy was Oscar's final order after surviving the sinking of three separate boats during the height of the conflict. Oscar lived out the rest of the war on land at the home of a sailor.

Reluctant Tourist

Cathryn Chartez liked traveling, especially with her feline companion. The pair went to Egypt for a holiday in 2002, but on the trip home to the States, the cat went missing. The search began, and Chartez enlisted the aid of airport police and staff to find her AWOL pet. Notices of the missing brown and white cat were distributed to no avail. Chartez had to board her flight without her faithful traveling cohort. Not giving up, Chartez booked a return flight to the land of the Nile two months later.

Less than a week after Chartez's arrival, the missing cat was found when an electrician discovered the feline trying to stay out of the rain near the airport. The united pair returned home without any more international incidents.

Pepsi that Purrs

One December evening, a tiny hum broke the silence as Julie Spence walked across the North Bay, Ontario, parking lot on her way to work, just two days before Christmas. Following the sound toward the Pepsi pop machine, the convenience store manager realized it was the purr of a cat.

After examining the area around the pop machine, Spence moved in for a closer inspection. After 45 minutes of spying through the flap where the pop comes out, Spence finally saw the kitten's head. Inserting her arm through the opening, the manager still couldn't reach the captive animal. Spence returned inside the store, and a customer came in to report a kitten was coming out of the pop machine. Spence adopted the abandoned, yet healthy, three-week-old white ball of fur that was only looking for a warm place to crash.

Courier Kitty

Communications between troops often proved perilous in some World War II situations. In 1942, during a siege in Stalingrad, a cat named Mourka carried messages across a sniper-infested street. The feline was able to deliver information on the location of enemy guns without detection. Why did the cat cross the road? To get to the food on the other side. Inside the building where the covert cat brought the classified information was a kitchen with a morsel waiting. Hunger outweighed the danger of being shot during the mission. Mourka's deeds were celebrated in a London newspaper.

Like Missing Luggage

Every comedian and frequent flier has a story to tell about a commercial airline losing a piece of luggage. However, reunification could never be as sweet as finding the missing feline contents of your luggage, tired and hungry but safe, after 21 days of separation.

Pumpkin, a 12-year-old orange tabby, was flying cargo class on a United Airline passenger flight from Germany to Washington, D.C., landing in England for the connecting flight to the States. The feline never made it, despite a search of the aircraft by the crew. Pumpkin's owner discovered that, in Munich, the cat carrier had broken, allowing an opportunity for escape. Three weeks after his mysterious disappearance, Pumpkin was discovered in Denver, Colorado.

The cat was treated for dehydration and extreme hunger and was offered a flight home inside the cabin of the aircraft. Of course, United Airlines provided the pillow and movie at no charge.

Who's Your Mama?

Cammie, a Georgia cat with a family of five kittens, was already busy providing the necessities of life for her babies when she took on two more mouths to feed. The feline's owner stumbled upon two abandoned baby squirrels at a construction site. With no mama squirrel to nurse the tiny, helpless creatures, the orphans were introduced to Cammie. The adoption was seamless, and Cammie's family expanded to seven.

The Monkey's Uncle

A 45-year-old Sumatran orangutan was suffering from depression at her home in a Florida zoo. Tondalyo had lost her mate and was lonely. Middle age prevented a move or the introduction of another mate. But it was a stray orange tabby that turned life around for Tondalayo.

A zoo employee introduced the pair, and it was love at first sight. The pair is inseparable, spending days playing, cuddling and napping together. TK—short for Tondolayo's Kitty—gave the orangutan a new lease on life.

Adoption Option

Whoever believes that cats and dogs are mortal enemies would change their mind after witnessing the loving generosity of this particular mother cat.

A Pennsylvania woman was trying to nurse a pug puppy after its mother had rejected it. Zoey, the resident cat, wasn't normally a big fan of dogs. But when her three kittens—roughly the same size as the puppy—would line up to be nursed, the unnamed canine would join in, and Zoey didn't complain.

Co-pilot Cat

Kiddo, a gray tabby, has the distinction of being the first cat to fly across the Atlantic.

American aeronaut and journalist Walter Wellman and five others left Atlantic City, New Jersey, on October 15, 1910, bound for England aboard the airship *America*. Unhappy yowling alerted the airborne crew that they had a stowaway. At one point, the noise became so unbearable that the crew considered transferring the cat to a boat. Poor weather quashed that notion, and soon the cat settled down.

Despite breaking the current record being in the air for more than 71 hours, the *America* crashed into the sea 475 miles short of its destination. All were rescued. Upon returning to the U.S., Kiddo became a celebrity in New York and, for a while, was available for public viewing at Gimbel's department store.

Wartime Wonders

It was a lean time for Londoners following the Depression in 1936, when a stray tabby seeking shelter tried to gain entrance to St. Augustine's and St. Faith's church. The verger turned the waif away not once, but three times. Undaunted, the feline gained entry and was discovered by Father Ross, who allowed the tabby to stay. After a fruitless search for its owner, the cat was named Faith and settled into church life with ease.

Faith was a good mouser and parishioner as she attended services, often sitting at the pulpit or in the front pew.

Faith eventually became a mother, giving birth to a black and white tom dubbed Panda.

In early September 1940, Faith stopped sleeping in her comfortable basket and would carry Panda to the basement. Deciding to investigate, Father Ross found the two cats curled up in a far corner of the dusty basement used to store old books and sheets of music. Despite numerous attempts to reunite the pair with their sleeping quarters, Faith insisted upon returning to the dark, underground room. The puzzling behavior would soon become clear.

Air raid sirens blared their warnings in London as bombs were dropped over the English capital. Father Ross was returning from Westminster when the sirens sounded, and he spent the night in a shelter. The next day, he was devastated to discover his church was one of eight that had been hit and sustained heavy damage. Firemen wouldn't let anyone enter the church to search for the cats; however, when they were called away, Father Ross ignored the danger and went to rescue Faith and Panda.

He found the pair in the basement where they had chosen to hide out for the past several days. The cats were frightened but unharmed, and shortly after the rescue, a roof collapsed where the cats had been hiding. Faith was recognized for her bravery and awarded a silver medal.

Bionic Sight

Ginger Snap doesn't know it yet, but the four-year-old auburn Abyssinian could become the first feline with a bionic eye.

The cat is part of a study group at the University of Missouri testing a microchip that may restore some sight to humans affected by retinal disease. Abyssinians are good candidates because they have a hereditary mutation that gradually causes blindness and can fall prey to retinitis pigmentosa as young as two years old, with a complete loss of sight by age four or five.

A silicon chip, about the size of the head of a nail, is implanted within the retina and contains thousands of miniature solar cells that transform light into electricity. The microchips stimulate the remaining healthy cells to improve deteriorating sight.

Humans were tested before cats, but feline subjects are ideal because their eyes are similar to humans' in size and design.

Earlier prototypes of the microchip have been implanted in cats, including those born blind, and researchers say the implant works, but they don't exactly know what the cats are seeing. Ginger Snap will receive the newest version of the implant.

By a Whisker

A bizarre case of revenge nearly claimed the life of Ashley, a Korat who lived in the English county of Essex.

One summer day in 2006, at Bradwell-On-Sea, a man operating a backhoe drove up to a house and started tearing it apart. While the demolition was taking place, a resident was in the house and narrowly escaped. In the rush to exit the dangerous situation, Ashley was left behind. The next day, the confused cat was located peering through damaged floorboards among the rubble. The feline was recovered without any injuries. Police caught up with the demolition demon who apparently had a quibble over money with the homeowners.

Mountaineering Meow
In August 1950, a group of mountaineers was preparing to scale the Matterhorn, a vertical climb of more than 14,000 feet in Switzerland.

Accompanying one of the climbers, Josephine Aufdenblatten from Geneva, was a 16-week-old kitten. To everyone's astonishment, the kitten followed the group each day as they made their way to a base hut just short of the summit at 12,556 feet. The last leg of the ascent was challenging for the young feline as it maneuvered to keep up with the mountaineers. The tiny four-legged hiker made the Swiss peak and then the Italian summit.

For the descent, the kitten was transported in a guide's backpack.

Rescue on the River

A precarious sight greeted passersby near a river in Missoula, Montana, in the early morning hours a few days after Christmas in 2005.

A cat was trapped on the ice and was crying for help. But the tortoiseshell was also imprisoned in an animal carrier weighted down with a large stone. It appeared that the container had been tossed over the bridge, but instead of landing in open water, it settled on the ice. The Missoula Fire Department and a rescue boat were dispatched to the emergency. After an uneventful rescue and a trip to the fire station, the severely malnourished cat was checked out and described as being "nothing but skin and bones." Rather than subjecting the stressed cat to an uncertain future, one of the rescuing firemen adopted the feline and dubbed the animal "Lucky."

War Rescue Mission

It's not known if it was business or first class, but 300 animals were airlifted out of a war zone in 2006.

When the bombing started in Lebanon, and Beirut was being evacuated, most pets were left to fend for themselves. The country's only three shelters sustained damage during the conflict, and the animals living under their care were relocated to a farm outside Beirut. Cat food was nonexistent during the hostilities, and it was an overwhelming situation for the volunteers. Finally, an American animal rescue group organized passage for 300 pets to the U.S.

Blame the Cat

The emergency caller from a Charleston Village residence in the province of Ontario did not provide a response to the 911 operator. The emergency dispatcher called back to check why the call was made and was told a cat made the call. The dexterous cat apparently walked across the phone, initiating the call. Police stopped by the home to check that the homeowner was okay and confirm the explanation provided by the owner. Police aren't buying the cat's ability to press three numbers and say it likely hit speed dial.

Super Survivor

The death toll was high—2400—after a 7.6 magnitude earthquake struck Taiwan on September 21, 1999. Thousands of homes collapsed, leaving 100,000 homeless. Rescue turned to recovery as people tried to deal with the aftermath of the massive disaster. The arduous task of cleaning up the destruction was into its 80th day when a cat was discovered buried alive beneath the rubble of a collapsed building. The amazing survivor was rushed to a veterinarian, where it recovered after being trapped for almost three months.

Homeless but Not Hopeless

A twist of fate in Florida brought together an abandoned kitten, a homeless man and a protester.

A small gray and white tabby kitten was seeking shelter in a bush from the pre-hurricane October winds in 2005 when a homeless man scooped up the tiny bundle. Ralph Caruso was unemployed and homeless, yet he felt compassion for the vagrant kitten and adopted the young feline, taking it everywhere he went in a small portable kennel. An altercation landed Caruso in need of medical care, but he would not go to the hospital without the kitten, which he had named Smoke. Paramedics relented and took the pair to the emergency to treat Caruso's broken arm.

Smoke waited in the cage while Caruso underwent surgery, and staff tried to find temporary shelter for the kitten. All of the animal shelters were full, but a chance call to Paws-2-Help found Eve Van Engel, who was living in a dumpster. The woman was trying to draw attention to the plight of exploding numbers of surrendered and abandoned pets by residing in a dumpster for a month.

A friend picked up Smoke and Van Engel's non-profit organization looked after the animal until Caruso recuperated and they could be reunited.

The French Connection

A Wisconsin cat made headlines when she turned up halfway around the world.

Emily went outside side as usual, but she failed to return to her home in Appleton near the end of September in 2005. A little more than three weeks later, the adventurous feline turned up in France.

While still in the U.S., at some point Emily had been investigating a container destined for overseas and unintentionally became part of the traveling cargo.

She was identified by her collar and offered a ride home by Continental Airlines. During the international leg of the flight, Emily apparently turned her nose up at the salmon she was offered, preferring to dine on French cat food.

Cat Burglar Bungle

Hefty Hercules was on the hunt for a free meal in Portland, Oregon, but he would have to break the law to satisfy his hunger. The 20-pound tabby caught the scent of some dog food but needed to break inside to get at the all-you-can-eat buffet. Hercules spied an animal door and stuck his head inside the flap. That's when the trouble started. It seems he had put on a few pounds and could not fit the rest of his body through the opening. Reverse didn't work either. Hercules remained stuck in the dog door until homeowner Jadwiga Drozdek rescued the feline. Hercules was turned over to the humane society until he could be reunited with his owner, Geoff Ernst. The portly feline had gone missing six months earlier when Ernst had traveled to Seattle for a lung transplant.

Prison Break

An American women's prison is paroling some cats, but not for good behavior. The mousers scratched some inmates, caused allergic reactions to others and, at times, were victims of abuse. Cats had roamed the grounds since the '80s; however, the prison became a dumping ground for unwanted cats, spiking the population. Many of the incarcerated women cared for and bonded with the cats. The warden agreed there were some benefits to having mainly feral felines at the institution, but the negative issues pointed to eviction. Most inmates were unhappy with the decision, because they had become attached to the critters and often contributed financially to the cost of their keep.

Spare No Expense

A cat wedding ceremony held in Thailand was a lavish affair. The feline bride and groom wore matching pink apparel for their nuptials in the country's hippest discotheque. The bill, which totaled $16,241, went to the cats' owner.

Cat-napped

It was a bizarre night for Zack, a gray and white longhair employed at Wake County Animal Control in North Carolina. Zack was hanging around the entrance of the shelter when someone snatched the handsome feline, stuffing him onto a bag. An eyewitness jotted down the license plate of the getaway vehicle, and made a call to police. The next morning, before the law could locate the thief's car or anyone at the shelter received that dreaded ransom call, the cat was returned.

Staff were thrilled with Zack's return, and he was back on the job testing dogs to see if they could be adopted by cat owners.

Canopy Caper

Mincho apparently preferred loftier accommodations when she hightailed it up a tree in her home country of Argentina and refused to come down. She remained in her tree penthouse until her death six years later. Mincho managed to have three litters while enjoying the high life.

Adoption Option

Female cats have expressed their maternal instincts with other species, usually something comparable in size to a kitten. But Satin, who had kittens at a Connecticut animal shelter, was quite happy to take on a six-day-old Rottweiler. Charlie was the only survivor when his mother gave birth to a pair of whelps. When there is a stillborn in the litter, the mother often rejects the remaining pup. Shelter workers tried bottle-feeding, but it was demanding and couldn't satisfy the pup's requirements so the pup was turned over to Satin. Satin embraced the new family member, as did her offspring. However, that will change because Rottweilers—descendents of Roman army camp dogs— can weigh in excess of 90 pounds when fully grown.

THE ABCs OF BREEDS

*God made the cat in order that humankind might have
the pleasure of caressing the tiger.*

–Fernand Mery

Best of Breed
There is no shortage of breed varieties when it comes to domestic cats, and I'll take one of each. There are more than 100 breeds, some of which have only made a brief appearance in history, and new breeds are just scratching to get out the door. And, some breeds may have two or more names.

Cat organizations and registries don't always agree on which breeds should be officially recognized, or on the color variations allowed for showing purposes. The Cat Fanciers Association is the world's largest pedigree cat registry. The organization does not recognize all pedigreed cats for competition purposes. Currently, they allow 39 different breeds of cats to compete in the Championship Class, one breed in their Provisional Class and one breed in their Miscellaneous Class. Still, the fur would fly if we didn't at least acknowledge as many breeds as possible.

A CATALOG OF CATS

Abyssinian
This sleek, muscular, shorthaired cat has an interesting past. During Queen Victoria's reign of the British Empire, the Emperor of Abyssinia, now called Ethiopia, proposed marriage to the female ruler. Instead of answering the lovelorn emperor, the queen chose to ignore his offer.

The African nation's leader was angered by the absence of a reply and ordered the arrest of all Europeans residing in Abyssinia. The British monarch reacted by sending a force of thousands to secure the release of the captives. The emperor took his own life as the troops approached, ending the possibility of a conflict.

British soldiers returning to England brought some Abyssinian kittens with them and selective breeding led to the establishment of this graceful animal. Alias include Ethiopian cat, Algerian cat, British tick and Somali.

Abyssinian Bobtail
This breed looks like an Abyssinian with an accoutrement on the tip of its tail. It is the result of a cross with the Japanese bobtail.

American Bobtail

Sporting a short tail with a cotton-ball–like feature attached to the end, the American bobtail has several stories about its background. The most accepted account resembles the adage of turning a sow's ear into a silk purse.

During the 1960s, a pair of tourists spotted a scruffy, vagrant male tabby kitten wandering in search of food. The little fellow was adopted by the couple and later mated with their Siamese female, producing some short-tailed offspring. A series of other matings provided the foundation for this official breed.

Owners sometimes claim that these cats are doglike in personality and lack true cat vocals.

The phrase "domestic cat" is an oxymoron.
–George F. Will

American Curl

No, it is not the name of a new hairstyle; it refers to a relatively new breed of cat with stylishly curved ears. The unusually shaped ears with outward-facing strands of hair look like they were designed by a couturier. The ears curl back, revealing a tuft of hair that normally resides inside the ear, only more pronounced.

The breed's origin is traced to a pair of kittens that showed up at a home in California in 1981. One of the kittens was a black female with long hair, and she sported an unusual set of ears. The homeowners kept the unique kitten, and when she reached maturity, she had a batch of kittens, half of which inherited the specially shaped ears. The mother cat and two kittens with curved ears appeared at a cat show in 1983, creating an interest among cat fanciers. Careful breeding led to an established breed. This child of the '80s is rare; however, breeding has expanded the variety of colors from the original homeless black kitten.

American Lynx

A pair of American cat breeders initiated this breed in the 1980s. Not much information is available about this feline except that it has a stumpy tail, and two tabby coat patterns exist for either a longhair or a shorthair cat.

American Shorthair

Formerly known as the domestic shorthair, this breed was given a new name in the '60s to elevate its significance and distance it from commoners—non-pedigreed house cats.

This noble breed takes its place among the pioneers that came to America on the Mayflower, earning its keep as a pest exterminator.

American Wirehair

This breed was established in the 20th century from a kitten with a distinct coat. Each hair on its body is shaped like a crochet hook. Born on a farm, the unusual kitten was brought to the attention of a neighbor who bred cats. Recognizing the potential for a new breed, the neighbor paid $50 for the kitten and began a serious attempt to establish a show contender.

Fortunately, its somewhat intimidating punk look is coupled with a sweet temperament.

Angora

Recorded as a distinct breed in its native Turkey during the 1400s, this plush, white longhair was often given as a gift to European families of nobility from Turkish royalty in the 16th century.

To an untrained eye, Turkish Angoras are easily confused with Persian cats. However, Angoras are distinguished by having shorter hair on the body and longer hair on the tail, underbelly and neck—like a three-piece suit of luxurious fur. The Turkish Angora was duplicated in the 20th century in Britain because breeders thought the Old World breed had vanished.
See British Angora.

Anatolian

This breed is also called a Turkish shorthair, and the preferred coat color for owners in Turkey is white. The eye color of the Anatolian can vary, but residents of this cat's native country prefer blue or green.

Applehead Siamese

This breed is not the product of the computer company but an attempt by breeders to resurrect the original body type of the Siamese. Less angular and with a round head, this breed is also known by other names including traditional Siamese, applecat, old-fashioned Siamese, classic Siamese and Thai cat. It is also sometimes referred to as an opal cat, so named because of its stunning blue eyes, which are reminiscent of the gem, against the backdrop of a creamy coat.

Australian

This mutant version of the Siamese breed is a rare cat with large ears, a long nose and short or absent whiskers.

Australian Mist

A kitten Down Under that differed in appearance from its littermates became the founding member of a new breed in the 1980s. This feline has a medium build with a pastel coat and a ghost-like tabby pattern. It was originally named "spotted mist," but the name was changed in 1998 because of the marbled coat pattern.

Balinese

This exotically named breed was a fluke of nature that originated in the U.S. In the 1940s, some Siamese kittens entered the world with more hair than what is customary for their breed, and rather than resorting to euthanasia or giving them away, one breeder decided to capitalize on the anomaly.

The name longhaired Siamese offended Siamese cat breeders, so the moniker Balinese was adopted as a suitable breed name because of Bali's close proximity to the birthplace of the Siamese—Siam (modern-day Thailand).

Bengal
This breed enables its owners to indulge their jungle fantasies with a domesticated version of a wild leopard.

The Bengal was born out of a scientific study on feline leukemia. A university geneticist crossed leopards with domestic cats, and the female hybrid kittens were bred back to domestic cats, creating a new breed in the '70s. The Bengal's richly spotted coat bears a remarkable similarity to that of its wild counterpart. These cats are known to like water, so wear a Kevlar wetsuit when taking a bath—they are likely to join you.

Birman
This mysterious, silky creature resembling a longhaired Siamese is linked with Burma. Bearing similar dark points on the head, legs and tail to a Siamese, the Birman's distinctive, white-gloved paws set it apart and tie into the legend of its origins.

Before the time of Buddha, 100 pure white cats were sentinels of the sacred Khmer temple on the side of a mountain in Burma. During an attack on the sanctuary by neighboring rogues, the high priest suffered a heart attack. A favorite cat placed his paws on the body of the dying man, and the soul of the priest was reincarnated in the cat, mystically transforming the color of its coat into its modern day appearance. Other priests observed the strange phenomena and sprang into action against their attackers, driving them away from the temple. The other 99 cats, too, had transformed their coloring and were forever known as the Sacred Cats of Burma.

While the legendary account of the Birman is awash in color and mystique, there is an information gap between the tale of the temple and the four versions of how the cat came to be established as a pedigreed breed in France in the early part of the 20th century. One account places an English officer in the midst of the Third Burmese War in 1885. He apparently warded off an attack on priests during the Brahmin invasion and was given a pair of cats as a reward for his rescue efforts.

In another version, a rebellion near a temple had priests packing up their sacred cats in search of safety. An Englishman and a Frenchmen aided the holy men in relocating to the Tibetan mountains. As a sign of gratitude, a breeding pair of felines was sent to France. A third story tells of a wealthy American who was traveling in the East. He managed to buy a pair of the sacred temple animals from an unhappy servant of the priests. A final and questionable version points to a pair of French breeders who selectively crossbred a longhair cat with a Siamese and then concocted an interesting background to elevate the breed's status.

Bombay

The only thing this feline has in common with its namesake is its likeness to the Indian black leopard. The panther-like cat with a shorthaired, jet black coat was bred in Kentucky—far from India—in the late '50s to perpetuate the color of its coat.

British Angora

You could call this breed a copycat. It is a re-creation of the
original Angora from Turkey. During the early 1960s, British
breeders wanted to revive the breed, because it seemed to have
vanished in the West. They were successful, but there are some
minor physical differences between the British and Turkish breeds.
Coincidentally, a few members of the original Turkish Angora were
found in its native country at the same time as the British
breeding program, and a population was reestablished.

British Blue

This hoity-toity beauty is all about the color. The popularity of
this plush, blue-gray version of the British shorthair has some
cat fanciers in the UK recognizing it as a distinct breed. In
Canada and the U.S., however, it does not have distinct breed
status and is still lumped in with the British shorthair.

British Shorthair

This breed's ancestors arrived in Britain with the Romans sometime after the first century AD and survived a turbulent history.
From keeping the rodent population under control to being the
target of torture and death by overzealous Christians, the British
shorthair was finally accepted as a delightful household pet in the
Victorian era. The preferred coat color among many breeders is
blue-gray, which, as mentioned above, has some breeders believing
the cat should be a separately named breed based on its color.

Burmese

Although this breed is believed to have inhabited Burma before
Columbus set sail, a clear record of its lineage does not exist
before the 1930s.

Mentioned in a poem that appeared in the *Thai Cat Book*, written
sometime between 14th and 18th centuries, the copper brown feline
was considered sacred in all the usual places—palaces, temples and

monasteries. This pampered and revered breed had student priests to attend to its every need. The priests maintained pure bloodlines by adhering to a "closed herd" policy and did not allow any breeding with non-Burmese cats.

Today's modern Burmese can be traced back to the efforts of Dr. Thompson, a San Francisco psychiatrist. Thompson acquired what was first considered to be a brown Siamese named Wong Mau. Further investigation revealed that she was the product of a Siamese-Burmese cross. Wong Mau was bred to a Siamese in 1932, and her offspring were the beginning of the modern-day Burmese.

Burmilla

This elegant breed of feline is definitely the lovechild of an odd couple. In 1981, an unexpected mating in Britain between a male silver chinchilla cat and a lilac Siamese produced beautiful kittens and was the beginning of a new breed. Both parents of the founding litter were supposed to have been bred with cats of their own breed instead of each other.

Burmoire
A deliberate cross between a Burmilla and a Burmese brought into existence kittens with phantom tabby markings. A new name for the breed was adopted—Asian smoke.

California Rex

An unusual find in a California animal shelter during the late 1950s laid the groundwork for a new breed. A female and one of her male offspring appeared different from the other cats because of their long, wavy hair. The pair was adopted, and because their coats were longer and wavier than those of normal rex cats, the mother and son were allowed to mate. Their progeny was born with longer and silkier hair. Originally dubbed the Marcel cat, the breed is referred to as California rex by many cat lovers.

California Spangled
Elaborate, handpicked matings among domestic cats from four continents produced, after several generations, a shorthaired, spotted feline that resembles a leopard. Controversy arose when the wild-looking new breed was introduced to the world and marketed through the mail-order catalog of a prominent American department store in 1986.

Ceylon

This breed was founded from a group of good-looking feral cats in Sri Lanka (formerly known as Ceylon). An Italian veterinarian traveling in that country took a fancy to the friendly, independent local felines, which mirrored an early form of the Abyssinian. He brought two couples back to his country and later imported a few more to strengthen the new breed, which Italian breeders embraced in the late '80s.

Chantilly or Tiffany
This dual-named North American cat isn't having an identity crisis; it was given the new name Chantilly after being known as

Tiffany so as not to be confused with a British breed with same name (but a different spelling)—Tiffanie. This beauty with golden eyes sports a longhaired, luxurious, brown coat.

Chinese
This is apparently a lost breed that is also an enigma. Starting in the late 1700s, different writings surfaced describing a black and yellow cat with pendulous ears. However, no specimens have ever been found, despite numerous efforts.

Chinese Harlequin

Not a romantic novel, only a romantic goal. This new breed was specifically mated to re-create an ancient breed that had the coloring of a Holstein cow—white body with black patches.

Colorpoint British Shorthair

Another new breed with a twist. Beginning in England during the '80s, breeders wanted the coloring of a Siamese without the bodystyle or attitude, so they took a basic British shorthair and augmented its appearance with a Siamese-like coat.

Cornish Rex
It was the era of rock' n' roll and poodle skirts when along came a poodle cat. Born on a farm in the county of Cornwall during the summer of 1950, one male red tabby stood out among a litter of five because its coat resembled that of a poodle.

The wavy-haired creature was sired back to his tortoiseshell mother for a chance at the genetic jackpot. Breeding improvements, to ramp up the animal's stamina, were achieved through selective mating with other varieties of pedigreed cats.

Coupari
British breeders gave this name to the longhaired version of the Scottish fold.

Cymric

Pronounced *kim-rick,* this breed is a longhaired version of the tailless Manx. Some cat associations call it a longhair Manx.

Devon Rex

A feral male with curly fur roaming around an abandoned mine in Devon, England, eluded capture and managed to sire a litter that produced the foundation for this breed in 1959. It was eventually discovered that the Devon had a completely different rex gene than its close neighbor, the Cornish rex. Both parents must carry the recessive rex gene to pass on the wavy hair. This breed has also been known to wag its tail like a dog.

Dutch Rex

A twist on the traditional wavy coat of a rex cat was first noticed on a single feline in the Netherlands in 1985. The kitten's coat had a coarser, bristle-like wave, unlike the fine, wavy fur of the Devon or Cornish rex.

Egyptian Mau

Closely resembling the felines depicted in Egyptian art, this spotted breed has two theories of origin. Most experts agree it is one of the oldest feline breeds; however, there are apparently two varieties, one developed through selective breeding and the other coming from the streets of Egypt.

The features accepted for showing stem from the breeding efforts of an exiled Russian princess. During the mid 1950s, Princess Nathalie Troubetskoy immigrated to the U.S., bringing with her a silver female named Baba and two other kittens to establish the breed in North America.

European Burmese

American cat fanciers are more rigid about what is acceptable for coat colors of the European Burmese for competition. Cat breeders in Europe are open to more color varieties such as brown, lilac, cream, red cream and seal tortie.

European Shorthair

This modern cat was derived from ordinary working and pet felines, but there are different definitions about what exactly is a European shorthair. It wasn't until after 1982 that cat fanciers made the distinction between the European shorthair and the British shorthair. The European shorthair's body is not as stocky, and it has larger ears than its British relative.

Exotic Shorthair

This is a feline whose good looks live up to its name. This shorthair variety of a Persian emerged in the 1950s and received the "exotic" designation from American breeders in 1966. Strengthening the bloodlines resulted in a beefy, docile breed with a shorter coat than a traditional Persian.

German Rex

The first appearance of the German rex occured in East Germany during the late 1940s. The homeless cat with wavy hair carried the same gene as the Cornish rex. Ironically, the Cornish rex wasn't discovered until the beginning of the next decade. The German rex appeared in European cat shows until the 1980s; however, in the last few decades, the line of felines is slowly disappearing in European competition rings.

Havana Brown

Despite its Caribbean name, this feline hails from England and was selectively mated in 1952 for its color. Breeders say it has no interest in people food.

Himalayan

Nicknamed "Himmy" in the U.S., this Persian in Siamese clothes is referred to as a colorpoint longhair in Britain. Despite breeding programs that date back to the 1920s in America, Sweden and Britain, this gorgeous feline still hasn't obtained breed recognition with some cat-fancier associations.

Italian Rex

A wavy-haired cat was first seen in Italy in 1950. It did not grab the attention of Italian breeders and vanished after the first generation.

Japanese Bobtail

Once they roamed the palatial homes of nobility in Japan, then they were allowed to go public in the 17th century. It was an act of need, not generosity because too many rodents were interfering with the commerce of the silkworm, and something had to be done. This ancient breed has both longhair and shorthair varieties.

Javanese

This feline is a spinoff of a Balinese with a Siamese look and a long, silky coat thrown in for good measure. It has nothing in common with its namesake country and came about by being a different color than its Balinese littermates.

Korat

The Korat hails from Thailand and has been held in high esteem in that country for centuries. During agricultural ceremonial rituals, Korats were paraded about after a dry growing season, and water was poured over them to entice the rains to come. A bride-to-be could expect a pair of Korats on her wedding day, symbolizing prosperity for the newlyweds' future. The silver-blue color of the Korat's shorthaired coat is linked to many symbolic beliefs within the Thai culture. One belief is that it represents the precious metal silver. Although one cat was exhibited in London in 1896, the Thai did not export their prized breed outside their borders until 1959.

Maine Coon

Described as the "first truly American breed," the Maine coon is a rugged, cold-climate, gentle giant that looks like a distant cousin of the Norwegian or Siberian forest breeds. There are no less than 12 possible theories for its origin. The majority of the stories point to American migration via ships sailing from Europe. Other explanations suggest the breed arose from cross-breeding domestic cats with wild ones.

Maine Coon Longhair

That's the suggested name for a Maine coon with a wavy coat. This cat carries the rex gene, which gives its coat a body wave, like a perm at the salon.

Maltese

From the 122-square-mile republic of Malta in the Mediterranean Sea hails a blue-gray shorthair that has been called several different names. François Moncrif recorded Maltese cats living on the island in the early 1700s in his book, *Les Chats*. The blue cat has been called and shown under the names archangel, Russian blue, Spanish blue and Chartreuse blue. It would probably be safe to say the Maltese doesn't care about its origins as much as humans do.

Manx

Recognizable because of the missing tail, the Manx is an old breed originally from the Isle of Man, located in the Irish Sea. The cat with no tail has many tales about why it is tailless. Some of the humorous versions include someone on the Ark shutting the door on the cat's tail and house cats mating with rabbits.

The Manx breed is most popular in the U.S.; however, at home on the Isle of Man, the Manx has reached iconic status and appears on coins, stamps and in advertising.

Mexican Hairless

The Mexican hairless bears an uncanny resemblance to the Canadian sphynx, with some minor exceptions, such as long whiskers and tufts on hair on its back and tail, which are shed in the summer months. An American couple living in New Mexico in 1902 received a pair from local natives, the only remaining pair of an Aztec breed, they were told. The male met an untimely death thanks to a pack of canines before he could sire any offspring. It is believed that the female was sold and was possibly sighted in a few European cat shows, but the trail has since gone cold.

Munchkin

This cat is the dachshund equivalent of the feline world. A fluke of nature rediscovered in the U.S. in the 1980s, the munchkin breed has both supporters and detractors. Munchkins were apparently seen at Madison Square Gardens in 1911. Reports of the low-rider cat were few and far between, and it seemed to vanish from the radar after World War II. In 1983, a pregnant stray munchkin was found in Louisiana and became the foundation of today's stock.

Munchkins have a regular cat body with shortened front limbs. Having stubby front legs makes them more cunning when trying to figure out how to get onto kitchen counters.

Norwegian Forest Cat

The Norwegian forest cat is mentioned as early as the ancient mythological tale in which the god of thunder, Thor, couldn't lift the heavy feline. And another Norwegian goddess had two of these hefty cats pull her wagon. Six theories for the magnificently coated breed's origin exist. One possibility is that Viking ships transported Scottish wild cats to Norway, a country without local wild cats, which were eventually bred with domestic cats to produce the Norwegian breed. Another theory traces Angoras traveling on trading ships from the Middle East to the Mediterranean up through various ports to Scandinavia, where they were mated with larger-framed cats to produce a bigger breed.

Ocicat

The Ocicat is a breed that almost never was. In the mid '60s, a program to obtain an Abyssinian with Siamese markings produced an unexpected result—a beautiful male with golden spots. Because the cat didn't have the desired look, it was neutered and sold. Several years would pass before another American took up the cause. Throughout the '70s and '80s, other breeders contributed to improving the type while another line of the breed was initiated in Europe. This breed is friendly and will shadow its owners as they move from room to room.

Oriental
Essentially, the Oriental is a Siamese without the markings or color points. A longing for a solid color Siamese, which dates back to the 1800s, was the motivation behind the breeding program that resurrected the graceful feline. Orientals like people and can acquire interesting habits such as being able to open purses and drawers in search of playthings.

Oriental Spotted Tabby
This striking Siamese-type comes with spotted tabby markings. British breeders were attempting to resurrect a simliar type to a wild-looking descendent of Egyptian cats.

Persian

Persians are the most registered breed with the Cat Fanciers Association and one of the oldest breeds. Historians have come up with nine theories about the feline's roots. One theory involves the invasion of several different Asian and Middle Eastern countries over hundreds of years.

It is speculated that when the Persian king conquered Egypt in 525 BC, trophy cats were taken back to Persia, where the harsher winters led to the development of the feline's thick, luxurious coat.

By the 17th century, the exquisite feline had been introduced to Europe, and soon many Europeans wanted an aristocratic animal that they could slave over daily with grooming tools. Most people in North America readily recognize the white Persian kittens used to advertise toilet paper in TV commercials; however, there are other color varieties for this breed.

Ragamuffin
Much mystery lies behind the origins of this breed. Said to have been split into its own breed in 1994, this longhaired, affectionate cat's genetic pool had begun with street cats 30 years earlier. This downtown-goes-uptown breed has several different color forms. The ragamuffin has a mellow disposition and is described as a people-pleaser.

Ragdoll
The ragdoll owes its name to its laid-back manner, particularly how it goes limp when you pick it up. There is some vagueness about its origins, but it is known to have come out of California in the '60s. This breed is reported to be the result of mating a Persian with a Birman. Weighing as much as 15 pounds, the ragdoll is one of the largest domestic cats.

Scottish Fold

"Who bent ye wee ear, lads and lassies?" might be the question you would ask upon your first sighting of a Scottish fold. With the tip of its ears folded forward, as if the cat had worn a ball cap that was on too tight, this Scottish-born feline is a breed that was founded on a spontaneous mutation. Cats give signals with their ears about their mood; humans can be at a disadvantage trying to read this cat's ear language.

Siamese

Royal cat of Siam and palace cat are a few of the monikers associated with this ancient breed. Numerous books are dedicated to telling the colorful history of its origin and the many legends and beliefs associated with the breed. One recurring tale of its importance to Siam's royalty bestows the feline with the ability to transport souls. The favorite cat of a deceased royal would be entombed with the body in a container that provided a challenging exit for the feline. When the cat emerged, it was assumed the departed soul had been reincarnated in the cat.

Selkirk Rex

A beefy model of the curly haired rex breeds was discovered as a kitten in the U.S. in the late 1980s. A keen eye and some selective breeding gave the Selkirk the start it needed to become a full-fledged breed. The Selkirk has longer hair than other wavy-haired rex felines. It is a cat with a coat that sheep would envy.

Siberian Forest Cat

Credited with being the founder of all longhair cats today, the Siberian forest cat is common to northern Russia and wasn't imported into North America until 1990. History recorded the breed around 1000 AD, and the Siberian appeared in many Russian fairy tales. Breeders claim the breed is suitable for owners that are normally allergic to cats. The feline seems to have lower levels of an enzyme in its saliva that prevokes a reaction among many allergy sufferers.

Singapura

Delicate and dainty, the Singapura is the smallest domestic cat and a symbol of its native Singapore. Despite its light weight—6 to 7 pounds for adult males and 4 to 5 pounds for females—it is muscular and athletic. It was sometimes referred to as a "Singapore drain cat" for seeking refuge in Singapore's drainpipes.

Snowshoe Cat

White feet distinguish this new twist on the Siamese look. The snowshoe is an American breed with a somewhat sturdy build and a beautiful color, which is the result of crossing a Siamese with an American shorthair. Another unique aspect of the snowshoe is the upside down "V" facial mask. Despite some opposition from a few traditional Siamese breeders, the snowshoe is gaining popularity through those dedicated to championing the breed.

Somali

A longhaired version of an Abyssinian, this breed is said to be an extrovert with an appetite for fruits and vegetables, but it has no connection to the country of Somalia. This breed's appearance on the cat scene dates back to the '50s and '60s, when

breeders would randomly get a longhaired kitten in a litter of a shorthaired Abyssinians. Often referred to as a perennial teenager because of its playful nature right through to late adulthood, the Somali is a flashy looker, and many clubs are dedicated to the breed.

Sphynx

How does a breed with next to no fur originate in the land of ice and snow?

Mother Nature produced a surprise in a Toronto litter during the 1960s—a cat with no fur, an anomaly that breeders definitely wanted to perpetuate. With deliberate and selective breeding, the genetic pool broadened to produce a sound and naked cat. Not totally bald, this breed has a fine, velvety down covering its body that, when touched, feels like a horse's muzzle. It's not unusual to see this breed at cat shows parading the finest threads.

Tonkinese

An American breeder wanting a feline with beauty and brains dedicated a breeding program to developing the Tonkinese by crossing a Siamese with a Burmese. The breed is named after the Gulf of Tonkin, which is in the region of Siam (Thailand) and Burma (Myanmar). Reference to the "Chocolate Siamese" is made in *The Cat-Book Poems of Siam,* which dates back to the 14th century. With a heavenly shade of brown coupled with dark color points, Tonks are hardly humble about their good looks. The original 1950s breeder, Milan Greer, discovered "that I had created a prodigy in fur."

Turkish Van

Need a partner for aqua aerobics? Then a Turkish Van might be the best feline selection. Native to the Lake Van area in Eastern Turkey, this breathtaking beauty is also called the "Turkish swimming cat" because of its legendary love of water.

Evidence of felines existing in the country for thousands of years came from an archaeological dig discovery where clay figures resembling women amusing cats were unearthed. The archeological timeline indicates that felines were likely in the country long before they were domesticated.

The white cat with auburn-colored head markings and tail was relatively unknown to the western world until 1955, when a pair of Vans accompanied two photographers home to the United Kingdom. The photographers began the arduous process of initiating a breeding program by acquiring more specimens. They also started trying to gain breed recognition.

By 1985, Vans had been introduced to America; however, six years later a film crew on location in Turkey discovered that the locals considered an all-white Van to be the true Turkish cat. Another defining feature of the true Van was one blue eye and one amber eye.

York Chocolate
A mysterious family tree randomly produced a cat that was named for its home state—New York—and for the splash of rich brown color on the large cat's coat. An untraceable family tree has kept the York out of the cat registries since its 1983 origin, and the tree is a sapling with just a little more than 100 cat members.

Designer Breed
Say goodbye to sneezing and itchy, watery eyes; science has leaped into the forefront of discoveries with the creation of a hypoallergenic cat.

A California biotechnology company tested thousands of cats, searching for the minority that don't carry glycoprotein Fel d1, which is the trigger of allergic reactions. The allergen can be found in a cat's fur, pelt, saliva, serum urine, mucous salivary glands and hair roots. Odds are that one cat in 50,000 will not carry the allergen. Even if the cat doesn't make your eyes water, the price tag might—at least $4000 per kitten—that is, if you pass the ownership screening process.

PAMPERED PETS

What's for Supper?

Despite a feline's penchant for rodents as "fast" food, owners spend a sizeable amount of money on cat food and edible treats. Gone are the days when cats had to fend for themselves for a decent meal. Worldwide, pet food is a multibillion-dollar industry.

The United States alone had a record year in 2005, tallying a staggering combined total of $14 billion for dog and cat food. Cats accounted for a little less than half of that amount.

An American working in England in 1860 is credited with the birth of commercial pet food. James Spratt thought better of his dog than to feed him old ship biscuits and baked a nutritious and thrifty version of today's kibble.

Australia

More than 64 percent of households Down Under have one or more pets. The cat population of 2.3 million falls behind that of dogs and birds, with fish being the pet of choice at 13.2 million in 2004.

Although cats are low on the totem pole, their owners shell out a sizeable amount of money on them. More than 1.5 billion Australian dollars went towards pet food and products. That is more than the country spent on foreign aid. Analysts note that there is increasing demand for pet food manufacturers to produce premium quality cat food and treats. An increase in the Australians' disposable income is likely a factor in rising cat expenditures.

Austria

Austrians love their kitty cats, with roughly 808,000 homes housing 1.5 million felines in 2003.

Brazil

U.S. pet food manufactures are looking twice at this South American country, as exports of cat and dog food exploded in value from $54,000 in 1992 to more than $7 million four years later. And that number continues to climb.

As three-quarters of pet owners move towards buying ready-made food for their cats, manufacturers are poising themselves to capture the increased market. Their biggest competitor in providing food is the Brazilian kitchen, where most meals for pets are still prepared. Although cats are slightly behind dogs as the pet of choice, there are approximately 7 million felines in Brazil.

Canada

Canada imports almost 90 percent of the food consumed by dogs and cats. In 2005, Canadian cat owners spent an average of just under $300 per animal on feline food, and the country imported $360 million worth of pet food from the U.S. alone. Statistics Canada, a government agency that tracks all kinds of data, says there are about 4.5 million cats in the country. Canadian pet owners contribute a whopping $1.5 billion per year to the pet industry with purchases of food, accessories and veterinary expenses.

Chile

Chile buys 80 percent of its pet food from neighboring Argentina and Brazil, with the U.S. capturing the rest of the market. Chilean pet owners, which comprise about half the country's population, spend $150 million per year feeding their four-legged companions.

Only one-third of the population buys prepared food for the country's cat population of 1.5 million. The other two-thirds mainly make home-cooked meals for their felines or feed them leftovers. Perhaps some good, red Chilean wine to wash it down, as well?

China

As attitudes change and the economy grows in China, so does cat ownership. The government has relaxed breeding laws, which has contributed to the increase in the population of 20 percent from 1999 to 2004. The number of pets in China hovers just under 3 million.

Whiskas is taking the cat food market by storm with the lion's share of the market in China.

Germany

In Germany, pet owners spent about $3.8 billion in 2004 to feed and accessorize their furry companions. On average, each pet-owning household spent about $94, but that amount is expected to increase.

Cat food is predicted to dominate the pet retail market. Bean counters are forecasting that yearly expenditures will exceed $1.4 billion and capture more than 35 percent of the pet market in Germany. The European country imports $48 million in pet food from the U.S.

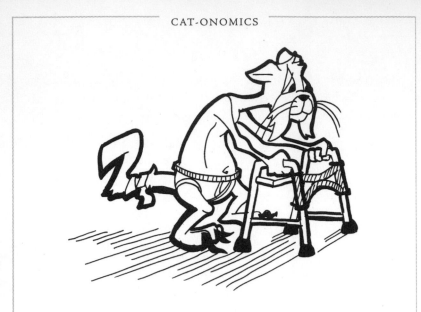

United Kingdom

With steady growth of cat ownership in the United Kingdom to the tune of 8 million-plus cats, feline food sales topped out at roughly $20 million in 2003. Quality food has increased the life span of cats, with roughly two-thirds of the cat population in their senior years.

Pet treats, too, are catching on with owners. UK cat owners indulged their felines with more than $1 million worth of treats.

United States

The United States likely takes the heavy petting award with more than 90 million pet cats, so you know there is a lot of spending going on. In 2001, pet food was an $11.5 billion-dollar business, including exports, and was approaching $15 billion in 2004.

From economical foods to water marketed for cats, Americans spend more on pet food than baby food. An estimated $38.4 billion was in spent 2006 in the pet industry on food, vet care, supplies, over the counter medicines, live animal purchases, grooming and boarding.

The *Super Market News* lists Friskies as the 10th most popular pet food in terms of sales, behind nine varieties of dry dog food.

Big Spenders

In 2005, 17 western European countries spent a combined total of €9.1 billion (about US $12 billion) on their pets. Those countries include Austria, Belgium, Luxembourg, Denmark, Finland, France, Germany, Greece, Ireland, Italy, the Netherlands, Norway, Portugal, Spain, Sweden, Switzerland and the United Kingdom.

Back to Nature

As a segment of the human population is moving towards organically produced food, so is kitty. Organic pet food demand grew by 63 percent in 2004, representing $14 million in sales, even though it accounts for less than one percent of total pet food sales.

Return to Sender

One of the largest recalls in the history of commercially pre-pared pet food occurred in March 2007 in North America. An undetermined number of cats and dogs in the U.S. suffered kidney failure and at least 14 died, prompting the recall of several brands of wet food sold in pouches and tins. Menu Foods announced the precautionary recall of 60 million containers of wet animal food. At least 42 cat food brand names that were manufactured and sold under private labels were removed from store shelves. The estimated cost of the recall is between $30 and $40 million. Menu Foods has three American plants and one Canadian manufacturer that collectively produced more than one billion containers of pet food in 2006.

WHAT'S IN THE BOX?

Kitty Litter

Cat owners in the U.S. spend more than $700 million on cat litter annually. Since its accidental inception by Ed Lowe in 1947, the discovery is one of the factors driving increased cat ownership. While working at his dad's business, which sold industrial absorbents, Lowe suggested using clay called fuller's earth to a woman who was fed up with the ashy footprints her feline left after using the cat box.

Will that be Clay or Pellets?

Ninety percent of kitty litters sold are clay based and offer a variety of features, such as clumping, odor suppression and dust control. Cats and humans sometimes don't agree on which type of litter will do the job. Some households use shredded newspaper, sand, wood chips, wheat or corn for filling the cat box.

Where's the Bidet?

Litter boxes come in different sizes, colors and styles, from open-air varieties to enclosed pans to ones that conceal their identity from humans, such as faux-potted-plant-shaped boxes.

Tidy Habits?

Cats cover their scat for a higher purpose than just to be neat and tidy. One suggestion is that, to avoid potential larger predators, they try to remove any sign they were in the area. Another school of thought says it is an act of subordination. By burying their dung, they suppress most of the scent, whereas a dominant cat may be so bold as to advertise its presence by not covering up.

Cat Litter Cake Recipe

You likely won't find this concoction in Martha Stewart's recipe book, and it is surprising that this cake hasn't shown up in a *Jackass* episode. Still, it is an edible, tasty version of what looks like a cat's litter box.

Ingredients
1 box of spice or German chocolate cake mix
1 box of white cake mix
1 package of white sandwich cookies
1 large package of vanilla instant pudding mix
A few drops of green food coloring
Twelve small Tootsie Rolls, or something similar
Serving dishes and utensils
1 new cat litter box
1 new cat litter box liner
1 new litter scooper

Method
Prepare and bake cake mixes according to package directions.

Make the pudding and chill.

Crumble cookies in a blender or food processor—just a few at a time. Add a few drops of the food coloring to one cup of the cookie crumbs. Mix with a fork or shake together in a jar.

After the cakes have cooled to room temperature, crumble in a large bowl. Toss with half of the crumbled cookies and enough pudding to make the mixture moist, but not soggy.

Place the liner in the litter box and pour in the mixture.

To get that authentic look, unwrap three of the Tootsie Rolls and heat in a microwave until soft and malleable. Form the ends of the Tootsie Rolls into a slightly pointed shape. Repeat the process with three more Tootsie rolls. "Decoratively" bury the rolls into the cake mixture.

Sprinkle the remaining white cookie crumbs over the cake, then do the same with the green-colored cookie crumbs.

Heat five more Tootsie Rolls until almost melted. Scrape them on top of the cake and sprinkle with crumbs from the litter box.

Heat the last roll until pliable and hang over the edge of the litter box.

Finally, place the litter box cake on a newspaper and serve with the pooper-scooper.

FELINE FASHION

Ring Around the Collar

Fashion for animals is a multibillion-dollar industry and no longer just for two-legged animals. From inexpensive nylon varieties to designer styles with diamonds, cat collars run the gamut in style, color and price. A collar with Swarovski crystals in a sterling-silver-plated setting, complete with a crystal buckle closure, is a bargain at $65.

Clothing

You can buy off-the-rack when it comes to cat clothing, or you can hire a cat tailor. There are outfits for every occasion, especially Halloween. It's pretty hard, though, for a cat to maintain a dignified look while dressed up like a frog.

The Cat Wears Dior

Every style imaginable is available if you want to drape your cat in designer threads. A fun-fur coat coupled with a matching jeweled collar and leash is a stylish look on the red carpet. Monogrammed clothing, designer labels and Halloween clothing are just some of the fashion items kitty can make her rounds in.

I'll Be at the Spa, Dahling

A beauty treatment at home is hardly comparable to the services of a professional. A wash and style is no longer the domain of show cats; all felines love to be pampered. Services range from basic grooming to ultra pampering such as pedicures and body massages.

Pet Bling in the UK

In the UK, pet owners spend a sizeable chunk of cash on luxuries for their pets such as trips to the salon, engraved brushes, jeweled collars, silver-plated bowls and play time with their cat friends.

ALTERNATIVE HEALTH TREATMENTS

A veterinarian is the first line of defense in a cat's health care, but as with humans, there are complimentary treatments available for felines. The treatments mentioned below are not meant as substitutes for veterinarian medical services but rather as complimentary treatments.

Acupressure
This hands-on therapy applies pressure at specific and targeted areas on a cat's body.

Acupuncture

This treatment is comparable to acupressure, only fine needles are inserted into the skin at certain areas to stimulate healing.

Aromatherapy

You won't detect the smell of tuna; instead, essential oils chosen either by the cat or the practitioner can be applied to the body. This type of treatment is used for a multitude of ailments, such as depression or fleas.

Crystals or Gems

No, kitty isn't requesting a diamond-encrusted collar. Energy released from select stones is said to have a positive effect on whatever the cat is being treated for. A gem can be worn or placed near the feline's sleeping quarters.

Feng Shui

Arranging your home to suit the cat sounds like a make-work project. The ancient Chinese practice of arranging your environment in a particular manner is meant to capitalize on creating harmony for the mind and body.

Herbs

Although cats are carnivores, they won't give up that status by using certain plants orally or applied to the body. The natural medicines are prescribed for a variety of recovery treatments.

Iridology

This eye-opening practice is used to diagnose a cat's health status by examining the iris for changes in color or shape.

Magnotherapy

You won't have to peel your cat off the refrigerator; rather, magnets are used on a cat to enhance healing by increasing blood supply to the affected spot.

Faith Healing
Healing powers are directed to the animal by the laying of hands on the afflicted part of the body.

Reiki

This age-old Japanese practice of touch healing can also be applied by placing the hands slightly above the animal's body to direct energy to a specific area. To make kitty more comfortable, many reiki therapists will go to its home to perform the treatment.

Crystal Ball Cat
Cat owners who really want to know what is on their cats' minds can call the Cat Psychic Institute. The business claims to have trained cat psychics on call 24 hours a day to answer the burning questions of cat owners.

Ultimate Bling

It is not uncommon to see humans with a trendy gold-capped tooth or police canines that have dental repair work done; now cats are going hip-hop with bling on their teeth, too.

Sebastian's owner, an Indianapolis area dentist, was concerned about his feline's under bite and the weakness it presented. As a proactive measure, he decided to apply his skills to remedy the problem. After a trip to the vet to anesthetize the cat, followed by quick 15-minute procedure on the teeth of the lower jaw, Sebastian had a million-dollar smile. Now, when the one-year-old black Persian smiles, the sunlight sparkles off two gold-crowned teeth.

The cost—$900 per tooth.

PET PRODUCT TRENDS

Plenty of Room at the Inn
More and more hotels across Canada and the U.S. are instituting "pets are welcome" policies. Some of the services the hospitality industry offers their feline guests include oversized pillows, check-in treats, robes, ID tags, turndown service and massage therapists.

Living Well
Self-flushing litter boxes and feathered French day beds are just two of the ways you can pamper your feline at home.

Stress Busters

While you meditate with yoga, cats can release pent-up energy at a feline spa equipped with a toy-filled gym and herbal catnip to enhance the experience.

Keep it Safe on The Road
Portable kennels are making room for harness systems that attach to your vehicle seat.

Trendy Kennels

If a survey of some Americans using boarding kennels holds clout, there could be upgrades galore. Here is a sampling of what owners want for their precious pets.

- Thirty-eight percent would like to see luxury suites equipped with raised beds, rugs and television.
- At least half of the respondents would like a service that provides Internet viewing access of their pet while they are away.
- Eighty-five percent said they want their cat to have daily one-on-one time from boarding staff.

Marriage Vows

"Do you promise to honor naptime and my favorite chair?" might be part of the nuptials recited during the marriage ceremony performed for a pair of cats in California. An ordained pastor, Dawn Rogers has tied the knot for cats, dogs and horses, and her fee for feline weddings is less than what she charges for the canines.

Cat Capitalism

Everything your cat could possibly want can be found at the Cat House Inc. It has Canada's largest selection of cat-related merchandise, with more than 5000 items. Since 1991, the Calgary, Alberta, outlet has been selling cat paraphernalia from recipe books and shower curtains for people to videos and furniture for cats.

War-Savvy Accessories

If Israel was attacked with biological or chemical weapons, cat owners could rest assured that their pets would be protected. Owners can purchase specially designed, pet-friendly gas masks, available in a variety of sizes, to guard against the inhalation of fatal poisons. Reasonably priced between $12 and $18, the short-term use gas mask will enable a safe evacuation.

Other protective products on the market include antibiotics to combat anthrax, tranquilizers to chill out upset pets and atropine, a remedy for chemical weapons.

Cat-centric Bling for Little People

One of the most successful companies designing and branding products for children is Sanrio in Japan. Their most recognized character is Hello Kitty, who made her debut in 1974. There are more than 2500 items featuring Hello Kitty, including everything from pencil cases to diamond watches.

Tick-Tock Goes the Cat Clock

Kit-Cat Klocks—with their rolling eyes and wagging tales—
have kept time since their creation on the west coast of the
United States during the Depression. Born to bring a smile to
those facing challenging times during the mid 1930s, the black
and white cat graced many homes and businesses, not only in
the U.S., but also in Canada. In the past seven decades, a Kit-
Cat Klock has been sold every three minutes.

Today, the company still manufactures the infamous timepiece
but offers a full range of colors. You can get a taste of nostalgia
by visiting their site at www.kit-cat.com

Policyholders

With American cat owners embracing medical insurance for
pets, yet another industry is expanding. Annual premiums range
in price depending on coverage, but the average cost is $275 per
year. Roughly one percent of cat owners have pet insurance.

Is That To Go?

For most doctors, the days of making house calls has long since
passed, but not for Dr. Ann Marie Roche, chief veterinarian of
a clinic in South Boston, Massachusetts. However, her visits aren't
for medical emergencies, but rather to curb the pet population.

Driving a specially equipped 21-foot van, Roche makes house
calls to spay or neuter cats. The service includes a physical
exam, surgery, vaccinations and a nail trim for a lower price
than if the animal was taken into some animal clinics.
The vet regularly travels to smaller communities with her mobile
surgical suite, performing as many as 20 operations per visit.

Diamonds Are Forever

Pet owners go to great lengths to preserve the memory of their departed pets, but one woman decided to wear hers. Sue Rogers of England paid $6500 to have a diamond ring made from the ashes of her pets. Carbon was extracted from the remains of her tomcat Patch, Lucky the sheepdog and a golden retriever cross named Sam to make the gemstone.

Travel Alert

These days, pets are logging almost as many air miles as humans, with 500,000 frequent fliers annually in the U.S. alone. From cargo to first class, frequent-flying pets face different standards with commercial airlines. Some airliners allow pets in the cabin for an extra fee, with some restricting pets to one animal per flight.

The Temperature Must Be Just Right

Furry cargo is not allowed in the belly of the plane on some commercial flights when the temperature is below 20°F or above 85°F.

Nasal Profilers

Because of a Persian's short nose, passage may be declined on some airlines because the animals have difficulty breathing at high altitudes.

No High Fliers

A sedated cat can't catch a flight with Continental Airlines, because they require a signed waiver indicating kitty is drug-free. Hopefully they don't ask for a urine test.

Money Moggies

Two cats, Brownie and Hellcat, hit the jackpot when their owner, Dr. William Grier of San Diego, California, left them $415,000 when he died in 1963.

Double Standards

The body overseeing pet travel in the U.S. requires a vet-issued health certificate for cargo passage but not if the cat is checked in as carry-on.

Your Papers, Please
Pets traveling with their owners in the European Union must have a document equivalent to a passport. The documentation required is the animal's tattoo number or microchip identification, vaccination and vet history. The goal is to ensure that animals are fit for travel and are up to date on their vaccinations.

Cat Café

Manhattan's Fifth Avenue in New York was the site of the world's first restaurant for pampered cats and their owners. Named Meow Mix Café, it opened for five days in 2004 with a menu of six flavors of cat chow. No dogs or catnip allowed!

MAY THE BEST CAT WIN

Ye Olde Cat Spectacle

The first cat show was more like a sideshow for hunting abilities; a record of prizes exists for best ratter and best mouser at the St. Giles Fair, held in southern England in 1598.

The First of Many
In the UK, the first official cat show was organized in 1871 at the Crystal Palace, in London.

Cat Fanciers Association Marks Centennial
More than a century of cat fanciers, dedicated to their breeds in every responsible and loving way, have participated in cat shows. Cat breeders and owners united to enrich and embrace high standards and animal welfare while infusing competitiveness into sportsmanship. The Cat Fanciers Association (CFA) has been one of the driving forces behind the development of breed standards.

A Legacy of Fur and Firsts

It was 1895 at Madison Square Garden in New York City, and there were 176 entries in the first National Capital Cat Show.

There were only three classes that lumped a few different breeds into the same category. The entries could be in one of the following categories: Longhair (any and all types), Foreign Shorthair (they lumped Siamese and Manx together in this class) and Domestic Shorthair.

Each cat had one shot at the overall grand prize, and the hardware went to Cozy, who was described as a brown longhair tabby neuter. The altered male, owned by Mrs. Fred Parker, would today be classified as a Maine coon.

A Movement that Started with a Purr

Over the decades, clubs and associations formed and cat shows flourished. In the 1950s, exhibitors were mainly women, and registration wasn't mandatory to be recognized as an "apparent purebred." The next five decades saw great strides in breed standards, health categories, show formats, expansion into other countries and other improvements.

Take Me to the Show

Five categories exist in competition—Kitten, Championship, Premiership, Veteran and Household Pet. Kittens vying for top spot must be between four and eight months old. Neutered or spayed kittens are accepted, but declawed animals are barred from competition in all categories.

Break It Down

The Championship class is for pedigreed, unaltered cats over the age of eight months.

The Premiership class sees competition among the altered (spayed or neutered) breeds.

The Veteran class is reserved for semi-retired, pedigreed show cats over the age of seven. Although they can compete in other classes, this category is not as stringent.

The Household category welcomes all cats, especially those beauties without a pedigree. Occasionally a pedigreed cat with a disqualifying feature, such as a Manx with a tail, will compete in this class.

Let the Games Begin

There are different levels among the Championship and Premiership categories and the judging ring is broken down further into two types—Allbreed and Specialty. The pedigreed cats are chasing points during the show season, aiming for the top award. Cat shows run almost weekly throughout the U.S., with Canada not far behind.

Color Blind

Color class judging takes a keen eye and plenty of skill and begins with cats of the same sex, color and competition level. To the untrained eye, they may all look similar, but it is the color of the ribbon that tells the real story. Blue is for first place, red for second and yellow for third. But that is only the first round of judging.

In the next level of ranking, the judge selects the best and second best of a color class, which is not necessarily all one color. Each breed standard dictates how many color classes are allowed. A black ribbon is for best of color class, and white is for second best. Once all the color classes of a pedigree have been placed, the adjudicator picks the best of breed and awards it a brown ribbon. The second-best cat receives an orange ribbon.

Cat Manners

Put hundreds of cats, their owners and exhibitors, trade booths, judges and facility operators in the same space together and you'll require some etiquette to maneuver through the feline frenzy.

- While cats compel us to stroke their svelte coats, it is better to ask the exhibitor for permission. Imagine 500 people wanting to scratch you behind the ears.

- Give exhibitors the right of way in laneways; they may be trying to get to the ring so Fluffy can capture first prize.

- Keep your wits about you and remain calm if you hear the dreaded "Cat loose" call. Hall doors will be closed, and if you see the escapee, just raise your hand so the handler can capture the runaway feline.

Call Me Cat for Short

Pedigree animals can compete with royalty when it comes to having several names. In the show ring, the long registered pedigree name is used, while at home a short version or the "call name" is used.

WE HAVE STANDARDS

Aside from the basic requirements—up-to-date vaccinations, good health and a clipped, clean appearance with every hair in place—the pedigrees must conform to standards specific to their breed. The Cat Fanciers Association recognizes 41 breeds, and the cats receive points based on conformity. Each breed has aspects for which a competitor will be penalized or disqualified.

Abyssinian

For one of the oldest breeds, judges are looking for an overall colorful cat with a ticked coat (each hair has bands of yellow, black and brown) and regal appearance. No pointy or square chins are allowed, but large, alert ears and almond-shaped eyes are two of the desired requirements. Points are divided among four attributes on its head, three body areas, the texture of its coat and the color of its eyes, coat and ticking. Abyssinians can be penalized for off-color pads and disqualified for having a kinked tail.

American Bobtail

Although it resembles a miniature version of a bobcat, the American bobtail's temperament makes it a good show contender, and it was accepted for registration in 2000. Points are distributed among five head traits, four different body areas and three for coat and color. The tail can determine whether or not a cat will receive a penalty. If the tail is too long or too short, the cat won't earn a ribbon.

American Curl

This breed made the leap from mutation to the show ring in a relatively short period of time according to registration standards. It is also distinguished in the Championship class because it is one breed with two coat lengths. Scoring for this cat is divided into five categories with 20 sub-categories.

American Shorthair

This breed has had success in the ring, with some feline competitors earning the coveted Cat of the Year award in 1984 and 1996. It continually makes the top 10 list of most popular cat breeds. The scoring breaks down into five sections: head, body, coat, color and eye color. Penalties are handed out for excessive cobbiness (stockiness) or a very short tail. Disqualification can occur if there is evidence of hybridization.

American Wirehair

This breed attained Championship status in 1978 and was honored with a National Championship Award in the same year. This cat is judged on four categories with an emphasis on its coat. A deep nose break is considered a trait to penalize, while an uncrimped coat warrants disqualification.

Balinese

This breed officially entered the ring in 1970, and five years later, a competitor achieved Grand Champion standing. Judging this feline breaks down into five categories and 15 sub-categories. The body structure and size is worth 12 percent of the evaluation. Burmese felines that exhibit crossed eyes won't win in the show ring. Disqualification factors range from illness or a weak back end to breathing through the mouth.

Birman

England recognized this breed in 1966, and the CFA followed suit a year later. It took only five years for a Birman competitor to achieve the Grand Championship title. Most breeders of this cat follow the French tradition of naming all the kittens born in one year with the same letter. For example, 2001 corresponded with the letter "y," so kittens born in that year had names beginning with the letter "y." All letters in the alphabet are used, and every 26 years the cycle begins again.

Judges look for a strong jaw with a firm chin and a medium-length Roman nose in this breed. Emphasis is placed on body type followed by symmetry of the cat's gloves. Delicate bones are not what the judges want to see, and if the gloves are missing on any of the paws, the cat could be disqualified.

Bombay

Sleek as night, the Bombay met breed requirements to compete in 1976, and one cat captured a national award in 1982. Twenty percent of the mark received goes to coat color. Ranginess is penalized, and too many toes will garner disqualification.

British Shorthair

Although relatively uncommon in the U.S., this breed is a big hit across the pond and appeared in the first UK cat show in 1871. The coat and torso are worth forty percent of the overall mark. A weak chin nets a penalty, and an incorrect number of toes is a disqualifying factor.

Like a graceful vase, a cat, even when motionless,
seems to flow.

–George F. Will

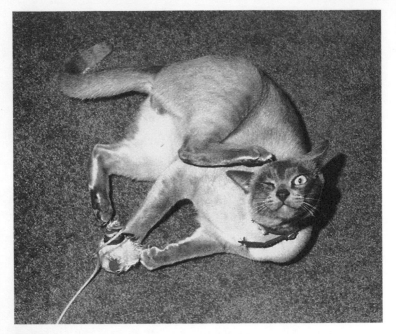

Burmese

Described as a dollop of joy, these beauties caused a stir in the '30s and '40s when the demand in the U.S. outstripped the supply. The CFA ceased registration for a while because some breeders, trying to keep up with demand, introduced Siamese into the mix. The breed was reinstated in 1957, but the cat must have three generations of pure Burmese bloodlines to qualify for pedigree status. Color is worth one-quarter of the possible 100 points in the show ring, and only four colors are sanctioned for this breed—sable, blue, champagne and platinum. Green eyes are a no-no, and the wrong color of nose leather is a definite disqualification.

Chartreux

Built for survival, the Chartreux was once lumped in with the British blue (and still is in the UK), but has since been recognized in the U.S. and Canada as its own breed. Texture of the coat is the highest point-getter in the ring. If the eyes are set too close together, giving the cat an angry look, a penalty is given. Green eyes are a disqualifying factor.

Colorpoint Shorthair

An elegant, modern incarnation of the Siamese, this breed gained show acceptance in 1964. This feline had only one coat color in early show days, but breeders have developed a larger palette for this breed that includes 16 different colors. A penalty is handed out if the paw pad color is not consistent with the individual's color description, and any signs of anorexia or white toes will get the cat disqualified.

Cornish Rex

Described as living art, this breed is popular at shows. According to the CFA, for a breed to be registered or recognized as such, there must be at least 10 different breeders working with it, and genetic information and historical background must be available. Taking only two years to leap from registration to show qualifier in 1964, the Cornish rex has a recessive gene that gives it the wavy coat. The penalty flag is waved for bald spots, and coarse or guard hair calls for disqualification.

Devon Rex

Developed from a mutation, the Devon rex has a different gene than the Cornish rex, though their wavy coats appear similar to the untrained eye. The Devon's coat has guard hairs, but they are weak and minimal in number. Judges will penalize for too small ears and disqualify for a bushy tail.

Egyptian Mau

The descendent of Egyptian cats, the mau swept numerous titles soon after obtaining CFA Championship status in 1977. A cobby or oriental-shaped body will have the judge marking the penalty column, and blue eyes are a disqualifier.

European Burmese

The name signifies that it is the CFA 10-color Burmese breed, advanced outside North America. This breed has 10 allowable colors, and its name sets it apart from the CFA's four-color Burmese. The popularity of this breed grew throughout Europe, Africa, Australia and New Zealand, propelling it to CFA Championship show status in 2002. Round eyes are cause for a penalty, and excessive tabby markings mean disqualification.

Exotic

This breed mirrors a Persian except it differs in coat length and the variety of colors permissible for show. Thirty percent of the judging points focus on the head. A kinked tail or the wrong number of toes yields a disqualification.

Havana Brown

If your fix is chocolate, then the Havana brown fits the description. This hybrid descendent of the Siamese is unlike its distant relatives. It gained entry to competition in 1964. Twenty percent of the marks are based on its color, and a cat with the wrong color whiskers will be disqualified.

Japanese Bobtail

This imperial feline has a shorthaired and a longhaired variety. Shorthairs received the CFA go-ahead for the ring in 1976, but the longhairs didn't receive their recognition until 1993. Body type takes precedence over color and markings for points. A cobby build results in a penalty, and a disqualification occurs if the tail lacks the pom-pom effect.

Javanese

Don't let this breed's refined appearance fool you; there is an athlete infused in the Javanese body type. Correct body structure and size, muscle tone, legs, feet and tail are worth 30 points. Penalties go to those with mushy bodies, and white toes are a definite disqualification.

Korat

This shimmering cat with five "hearts" also has heart. The first "heart" is the Valentine-shaped head; the second heart shape can be seen from an overhead view of the head; the third heart is disguised as a nose; the fourth is seen on the chest muscle while the cat is sitting; and the final heart is the one inside. This breed achieved Championship status in 1967, with a Grand Champion title following not long after. Twenty-five percent of the points are focused on the head, while another 25 percent are based on color. Any color other than silver-tipped blue calls for disqualification.

Laperm

From cute spiral-like curls on a longhair to a tight wave on the shorthair, the laperm's coat is an open invitation to constant petting. As of 2000, the CFA accepted it as a breed in their Miscellaneous class. You've got to have those ear furnishings (corkscrew ringlet hair at the base of the ear) if you don't want to be penalized. Short legs are not acceptable.

Maine Coon

These gentle giants were exhibited at the first American cat show in 1898 and won—under a different identity. Maine coons are the second most popular breed registered. Their coats must be even overall or they will be penalized, and if they have too many toes, they will be disqualified.

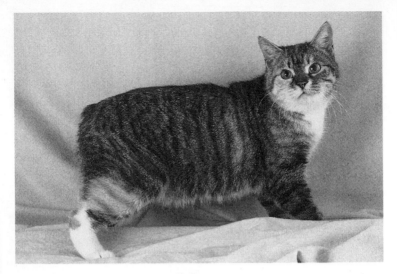

Manx

Unique in body structure, not all Manx cats are tailless—a characteristic they are known for. But for show purposes, the cat being exhibited must have been born without a tail and docking is not tolerated. The longhair Manx must have a dense coat or a penalty will be given. Evidence of hybridization is reason enough for the cat to be disqualified.

Norwegian Forest Cat
Captured in Norwegian fairy tales as "huge and furry troll cats," this breed is lovingly nicknamed the "wegie." A European cat registry gave it the nod in 1977, but it would be more than 15 years before it was granted CFA acceptance in 1993. Half of the show points are dedicated to the head—nose profile, muzzle, ears, eye shape, eye set, neck and chin. An overshot chin is cause for disqualification.

Ocicat

Wild in appearance, the Ocicat, oddly enough, received registration status in 1966, but it would take another 20 years to establish the breed and achieve competition entrance.

This cat's most important feature is its thumbprint-sized spots, which can earn it one-quarter of the points in the ring. Blue eyes or long hair are disqualifying factors.

Oriental

Sometimes referred to as a "Siamese in designer genes," the Oriental breed shows in an array of colors. Judging occurs in shorthair and longhair classes. A cat with the wrong toe count is automatically dismissed from the competition.

Persian

With more than 100 coat colors and patterns, this breed had been separated into several divisions by the CFA. The biggest emphasis in judging is place on conformation of the body structure according to breed standards, with almost 50 percent of total points going to the head, eyes and ears. A kinked tail, crossed eyes or weakness in the hindquarters mean disqualification.

RagaMuffin

Luxury on four legs, the ragamuffin is one of the newest breeds to receive CFA recognition. Reaching maturity by four years of age, this breed is penalized for having a Roman nose, small ears or a short tail. Too many toes or crossed eyes will get this feline disqualified.

Ragdoll

With four coat patterns, each with six colors, this breed offers visual variety. It received Championship status in 2000, and a competitor must have at least three generations of ragdolls in its family tree. Forty percent of the marks are focused on its head. Cobby bodies and a Roman nose signal a penalty, but eye color other than blue results in an exit from competition in this class.

Russian Blue

The Russian blue appears to have been dusted with icing sugar, giving its plush coat a frosted appearance. It has been registered for more than 50 years. A blue coat is a must for qualifying in competition.

Scottish Fold

The most distinguishing feature about this cat—its ears—is the reason it was developed as a breed. Competition status was granted in time for the 1978 show season, and the Scottish fold captured a national title the following year. The ears garner 25 percent of achievable points. A brow ridge can cost the cat a penalty, and splayed toes are a competition no-no.

Selkirk Rex

Born with a body wave, this breed obtained Championship status in 2000. Almost one-third of the 100 points is dedicated to the texture, curl and density of the coat. Judges will penalize for a cobby body and disqualify for polydactyl feet and lack of coat curl.

Siamese

Arguably one of the most recognizable breeds, the Siamese was a participant at the first English-organized cat show in 1881. Its genetic gold mine has been used in the development and maintenance of many other breeds. Color and body shape take the lion's share of points when judging the Siamese. The only eye color acceptable is blue, and a cat with off-color nose leather or paw pads will be penalized.

Siberian

A breed that's been around for centuries, the Siberian became more accessible to North America after the collapse of the USSR and the expansion of free trade. It was registered in 2000 and can compete in the Miscellaneous category, for now. A cat will be withheld from competition for a kinked tail and crossed eyes, and an animal that is the incorrect weight will be assessed a penalty.

Singapura

This tiny bundle of joy passed through the CFA's screening process and achieved Championship status in time for the 1988 show season. Although its population is relatively low, it has brought home the hardware in several levels of competition. Coat color, ticking, face and leg markings are worth 30 points. Any gray tones in the coat or undercoat next to the skin is cause for a penalty. A crooked tail and any color other than sepia agouti is definite cause for disqualification.

Somali

Often described as a medium sized, longhaired version of an Abyssinian, the Somali holds its own despite being genetically the same. It received the right to show in 1979 and took the Grand Championship and a national win in the same season. The length and texture of the cat's coat can earn it 20 points. Penalties arise over coat color and pattern faults. A cat will be disqualified if white appears anywhere in its coat other than on the upper throat, chin and nostril area.

Sphynx

All purr and no fur is a common description given to the
sphynx. Despite having the hairless gene, it does have "peach
fuzz" covering its body. One of the most unusual breeds, it
gained show status in 2002. Points for this cat are divided
almost equally among the head, body and coat. Hair other than
the downy type or bowed front legs constitutes a penalty, and
a cat with an abnormal tail or body structure will be disqualified.

Tonkinese

The Tonkinese was competing in Canadian cat shows almost
15 years before it was granted CFA Championship status in
1984. Since then, it has won many prestigious titles. Ranginess
and round eyes merit penalties, and a competitor faces disqualification if it has tail faults, such as a kink, or crossed eyes.

Turkish Angora

CFA-registered Turkish Angoras can trace their ancestry back to the country of their namesake. This breed was approved for Championship status in 1972, won its first Grand Championship title in 1975 and secured a national title in 1986. In judging, 40 percent of the marks focus on the head, ears and eyes. A coarse appearance is cause for a penalty, and a cat with crossed eyes, a cobby body or a kinked tail will get the disqualifying nod.

Turkish Van

A cat that has been known to enjoy water, the Turkish Van has been around for centuries. According to breeders, the Van takes three to five years to mature. It received Championship status in 1994. Penalty factors include cobbiness and a flat profile. A cat is disqualified if it has no color on its tail or head, or if there is color on more than 20 percent of its body.

IT'S ALL ABOUT THE COLOR

Coat Color and Patterns

Coat color and patterns don't constitute a breed but could be a definitive factor in distinguishing a breed. In the show ring, the palette that covers a feline's body is specific and well defined. Going back to the beginning of cat domestication, the basic template responsible for the rainbow of choice in color and patterns today is the brown mackerel tabby. It is also the foundation of the seven ancient mutations: longhaired, shorthaired, solid color, dominant white, white spotting, sex-linked orange or red, and the dilution factor (a gene that expresses the intensity of a color in a cat and influences a number of colors and patterns).

One with Color

Solid coloring exists when only one color with absolutely no markings is consistent all over the body. The fundamental colors are black, white, cream, and silver.

Not Too Shabby if You Are a Tabby

Competitive shows recognize five tabby patterns: mackerel, classic, spotted, ticked and patched.

Tone It Down

Dilute is a term often used when referring to paler versions of certain pedigree color patterns, such as a dilute cameo.

Just a Shade

Shaded patterns have three basic groupings: chinchilla, shaded and smoke. They share the distinction of having color at the tips of the hair, with a pure white undercoat.

You Look Marvelous

Parti-colors are influenced by the sex-linked red gene. The classic example and a popular choice among owners is the tortoiseshell. Essentially, it is a black coat splashed with random patches of red.

It's in the Genes

The Siamese gene is albino and influences where and how much color is expressed. The coolest parts of the body receive the dark color—the tail, feet, ears and eyes.

SPIN THE CRAZY COLOR WHEEL

Agouti

Agouti refers to individual hairs that have bands of black, brown and yellow coloring. The name agouti is shared with a sizeable South American rodent that exhibits the same coat pattern. Most Abyssinians have an agouti coat pattern.

Atabi

Also the name of a silken fabric with wavy, symmetrical markings that is synonymous with Baghdad, atabi is believed to be the source of the feline coat definition "tabby."

Auburn

This golden brown color is uncommon among felines. The Turkish Van's extremities have this color.

Blue

It doesn't mean you are sad; rather, it refers to any shade of stone cold gray.

Chinchilla

The cat that wears this coat is the envy of the ball. Its translucent, silvery color comes from individual white hairs tipped with black. The name was selected because the coat resembles that of a South American rodent. True Chinchilla cats have green or blue-green peepers. Chinchilla Persians corner the market for their stunning good looks and have been around since the late 1880s.

Chintz

Like the brightly colored fabric, this term refers to a modern-day calico cat. More than century ago, it was a name for the tortoise-shell-white Persian.

Chocolate

This color, which resembles the rich shade of milk chocolate, can be found in the American-resident Burmese and Tonkinese.

Cinnamon

This auburn or sorrel shade has been noted in several breeds.

Ebony

Another name for black, it is used in the U.S. to describe certain types of modified black-colored cats in the Oriental shorthair class.

Fawn

Unlike the creature of the forest, fawn refers to a light pinkish color.

Ginger

As a color, this term seems to bring confusion. It was used to mean yellow, then orange and finally marmalade. Breeders call it red because the gene responsible for the color removes black and brown pigments from the cat's hair.

Golden

This color occurs when there are black-tipped, golden hairs or brown-tipped, white hairs.

Gray

Although it is a common color, the term is never used. See "Blue."

Harlequin

Having a harlequin coat can mean a life full of romance and color, just like the widely read novels. A cat with this type of coat has a bicolored body that is 50 to 75 percent white with 25 to 50 percent color.

Lavender

This pinkish gray (or dilute chocolate) color is as heady as the smell of the flower. The name is sometimes interchanged with lilac at cat shows.

PET POPULARITY

This Is Not David Letterman's Top 10
The 10 countries that rank the highest in cat ownership are the U.S., China, Russia, Brazil, France, Italy, the United Kingdom, Ukraine, Japan and Germany.

The estimated world population of domesticated cats is 400 million.

Monarch Moggies

The Great Britain Association of Pet Food Manufacturers depends on crunching numbers for their industry. In a 2004 census, the estimated population of felines was just 500,000 short of 10 million. The majority of cats—92 percent—are non-pedigreed, but their lack of papers doesn't seem to affect their popularity. Thirty-one percent of owners say the biggest reason they keep moggies is love. More than half the households in the UK have cats.

Land of the Rising Cat

Though dogs currently lead in popularity as pets, Japan's cat population is roughly 8.4 million. One report indicates that in 2004, there were more dogs and cats than there were children under the age of 15.

North and South

Cats have been considered lucky in both Koreas. It is estimated that there were about six million pet owners in 2004. However, 77 percent of the pets were dogs, with cats trailing at 23 percent.

Communist Cats

Pets are popular in Russia and the reliance on commercially prepared cat food in urban areas is increasing. The estimated cat population is 12.7 million.

Cat status in Greece

Cats came of age as pets in Greece in the last few decades when they were welcomed into homes instead of being just a part of the landscape. Western influence opened the door to cats becoming pets and, in some eyes, status symbols. No longer do cats have to rely on receiving table scraps al fresco. Greek pet owners imported $1.57 million in pet food from the U.S. in 2003. And, America is only their secondary provider. The future looks promising for feline owners to lavish their cat with gifts as pet supply store openings continue to grow at a rate of 5 to 10 percent annually.

Cats in Belgium

Almost 25 percent of the households in Belgium—a small European country with a population of 10.1 million—have cats. Felines outnumber dogs, and in Brussels, there are almost three times as many cats as dogs. Ease of care is one of the factors contributing to the country's climbing cat population of 1.7 million. Belgians love their felines, and it shows when you compare the number of cats in Belgium with the number of cats in neighboring countries. There are 16.3 cats for every 100 inhabitants in Belgium, 14.4 for the Dutch, 12.5 for the British and 8.4 for the Germans.

Japan

It may be a coincidence, but in Japan cats arrived at about the same time as Buddhism. They were immediately recognized for their rodent-hunting skills, and Buddhist monks had at least two cats each to ensure mice did not destroy their sacred documents. Soon, commoners and royalty alike cherished the animals, believing them to be creatures of beauty. A small part of the population, however, associated cats with bad omens and demons. Most Japanese today revere felines.

Let's Have a Parade
Back when Thailand was known as Siam, cats were highly regarded. A celebration for the new king included a parade in which a cat riding in a chariot led the procession.

Floating Felines

Amsterdam is home to a cat shelter that doubles as a tourist attraction. The "Pussycat boat" or *De Poezenboot*, as it is known in the Dutch city, is a permanently docked barge and houses abandoned, ill and unwanted felines. A cat lover established the shelter in 1969; word spread, and soon people were flocking to see the floating sanctuary. The cat population increased, and a second barge became necessary. The first barge is now akin to a hospice for the aging and sick, while the other flat-bottomed boat is home to healthier and younger cats. With an escalating stray population—about 50,000 per year—it's no wonder a third barge is being sought by the volunteer group.

POOR KITTY

 Not everyone views felines as companion animals. Some cultures consider them livestock and fit for consumption while others harvest their fur.

Fact and Fiction
Not only did Charles Dickens include a passage in *The Pickwick Papers* in 1836 that refers to kitten-filled pies being sold as ordinary meat, but also in 1885, an English newspaper reported a woman was charged with catching and butchering cats, then passing them off as rabbit meat.

Fur Farms
The merchandising of cat fur is legal in some countries, banned in the U.S. and found repugnant in Canada and parts of Europe. Still, the industry continues to thrive. The pelt of a cat, used for human garments, blankets and toys, can sometimes be difficult to distinguish from other species without the benefit of DNA testing.

Australia's Surplus
It has been reported that the growing problem of feral cats in Australia has led to Aboriginals trapping and eating them. Stray felines have severely decreased the population of prey that would normally be part of the Aboriginals' diet. Victoria State, however, has banned dining on cat or dog.

European Ban
Many European countries have outlawed eating cat, but poverty, not tradition, is often a driving factor behind the culinary choice. The growing number of stray cats in some countries also contributes to the "waste not, want not" mentality associated with eating cat.

Don't Blame Asia

Thoughts of people consuming cats have Westerners looking east to Asia. While a minority of people in China, Korea and other Asian nations consider cat meat an acceptable meal, the practice has also been carried out in countries such as Switzerland, France and Britain.

Swiss Culinary
Despite a ban on trading and distributing pet meat in Switzerland, consumption is allowed. An occasional meal consisting of cat or dog is more likely to be found in the rural areas of the country.

Fast Food
In 1871, food was scarce in Paris while the French where at war with Prussia, and some meat markets did not hide the fact that they sold exclusively cat, dog and rat meat.

Roof Rabbit

In England during World War II, food was rationed, and felines were sometimes substituted for rabbit in meat pies.

CAN YOU HAVE TOO MANY CATS?

Multitude Mayhem

In the U.S., at least 700 cases of animal hoarding are brought to the attention of the courts and media every year. Horrific and deplorable conditions for animals and humans alike are often discovered at the residence of a hoarder. Most animals found in these environments are euthanized because of malnourishment, illness and other assorted problems. The humans responsible are often charged with cruelty to animals and, in addition, the court may order the accused to undergo a psychiatric assessment. While hoarding occurs with a variety of companion animals, cats and dogs are the usual victims.

Profiling a Hoarder

To understand the problem, an American interdisciplinary group called the Hoarding of Animals Research Consortium was formed in 1997. They define a hoarder as someone who amasses large numbers of animals that overwhelm their ability to provide even the basics of care. The hoarder fails to recognize the failing condition of the animals and environment.

Experts compiled information about characteristics from cases of animal hoarding that indicates about 75 percent of hoarders are women and roughly half are older than 60 years of age. Most animal hoarders are unmarried and more than 50 percent live alone. In roughly 69 percent of cases, animal urine and feces could be found in large amounts throughout the home, and in at least 25 percent of the incidents, the hoarder's bed was also covered with animal excrement.

Animal hoarding may be a symptom of underlying psychological problems.

Doctor Intervention

Experts say veterinarians may be unwittingly enabling hoarders, and the animal professionals are encouraged to watch for danger signs in their clients. Some of the signs include traveling great distances and at odd hours, bringing in a presentable animal and asking for extra medication to take home, being unwilling or unable to indicate how many animals they own and using multiple clinics.

Law and Order

Because many hoarders are repeat offenders, Illinois became the first state to address the growing problem in 2001. Lawmakers built several components into their law for prosecution by defining an animal hoarder, increasing penalties and recommending psychiatric help for the offender.

Cat Comedy

An Edmonton, Alberta, playwright has written a comedic play, called *House of Cats,* about two elderly, eccentric, cat-hoarding sisters. The two-act production ironically doesn't use any cats for the performances.

Lifetime Ban

A Calgary, Alberta, woman who pleaded guilty to neglecting 96 cats in her home is facing $20,000 in fines and a lifetime ban on owning pets. Police, following a tip, found 97 cats and one dog living in the house. There was no sign of food or water, and the inside of the home was littered with animal scat. All but one of the cats had to be put down. The provincial Animal Protection Act clearly states pet owners must provide enough food, water, shelter and space for their animals.

CAT TALES

How the Cat Got Its Purr

According to an old folk tale, the beguiling sound was given to the cat thanks to the efforts of three felines that helped a fair maiden perform a task for love. In the tale, a princess was required to spin 10,000 skeins of linen thread within a month to spare the love of her life from death. Faced with a time-consuming task and an unreasonable deadline, the princess enlisted the aid of three cats.

The 30 days passed, and the challenge was completed. The princess saved her lover, and the pair was reunited. As a reward for their tireless efforts, the princess gave the cats their purr, which resembled the sound of the spinning wheel.

Lucky 14

Dinner groups comprised of 13 people need not be superstitious about potential bad luck when dining at a particular London hotel. The Savoy has a famous wood carving of a cat named Kaspar that they seat on the 14th chair of a 13-member group. The number phobia is partly derived from a Norse myth in which 12 gods at a feast are joined by a bad spirit that causes problems, and 13 is also associated with the number of guests at the Last Supper. The Savoy superstition was further entrenched when a last-minute cancellation compelled one of the guests to sit in the 13th chair as host. He was later shot to death at his office.

Kasper was created in 1926 by Basil Ionides and has dined with many famous people, including Sir Winston Churchill.

One-Upmanship

An old Greek tale tells of the creation of animals by the sun and the moon. The sun made the lion, and the moon went one better with the creation of a cat—an animal more useful to humans.

To Kink a Tail

Siamese are known for their kinked tails, though breeders in the U.S. and Britain currently strive for straight tails. According to legend, the royal women of Siam would remove their jewelry before bathing and place them on the tail of the cat for safekeeping. To keep the valuables in place, the cats would kink their tails.

Cinderella Owes Her Fame to Cats
Several cultures had fairy tales long before Cinderella with a similar plot.

The Italians tell a tale of Cinders-Cat, a pretty, kind girl who was treated badly by her family and forced to wear the skin of a cat for clothing. Her name came from where she slept at night, on the floor next to the fireplace. She had a better life after meeting a handsome, wealthy man whom she wed. The English spin calls the female heroine Catskin.

The Danes told of a girl who was punished for feeding milk to stray cats. Despite a thrashing, she fed the next hungry cat that came calling. The feline grew so large after lapping up the milk that it removed its fur for the girl to wear as a coat. The cat continued to furnish the young woman with beautiful clothing and finally changed into human form. He was the brother of the king, and, of course, they got hitched and lived happily ever after.

Stradivarius Prodigy

In the rhyme "Hey diddle diddle, the cat and the fiddle," the cat must have played some tune to get that cow to jump over the moon.

 Nursery rhymes have been handed down through generations and shared among cultures, and among them, cats have received star billing.

Where Strings for Mittens Came From

The trio of juvenile cats that lost their mittens was likely the cue for mothers to attach strings to the winter apparel. In the rhyme, the punishment for losing their hand garments would exceed cold appendages; the three little kittens would miss out on pie. Fortunately, the kittens found their mittens so they would not be denied their pie.

Johnny Green Was the Poster Boy for Animal Cruelty

"Ding dong bell, pussy's in the well" is a testament to the actions of unsupervised children. The villain in this rhyme put a hard-working cat down a well, and Tommy Stout recovered the body.

Don't Be Cruel

One rhyme gives explicit instructions on kindly behavior towards cats:

> *I love little Pussy,*
> *Her coat is so warm,*
> *And if I don't hurt her,*
> *She'll do me no harm.*

See Puff Run

Many baby boomers will recall Puff the cat from their first grade reading books. Created in 1917 by Scot Foresman, child characters Dick, Jane and Sally were often found running with their pets in the book *We Look and See.*

Royal Mouser

This quartet of rhyming sentences tells of the curious Pussy Cat that travels to see the Queen of England. While catching a glimpse of her highness, the feline spots a mouse, which she frightens away.

Pussycat, pussycat where have you been?
I've been to London to see the Queen.

Pussycat, pussycat what did you there?
I frightened a mouse under her chair.

Count Catula

Although admired by the Japanese culture, cats had a dark side in some of the country's ancient beliefs. Vampire cats were the equivalent of the bogeyman; they could steal the identity of their victim. One of the better-known tales involves a prince and his love, O Toyo.

At the stroke of midnight, a vampire cat killed O Toyo while she was asleep in her room, before she could even get out a scream for help. The demon feline hid the woman's body and took on her form. With the prince none the wiser, each night, the vampire cat would go to him and slowly drain his blood. As he became weaker with no explanation for his illness, 100 servants were ordered to keep watch over him while he slept. The vampire cat cast a spell on the observers, causing them to fall asleep, and continued to steal blood from the prince.

As the prince's condition worsened, a priest began praying. A soldier by the name of Ito Soda interrupted the priest and asked to be assigned to guard duty over the prince. That night, while the other watchmen fell asleep from the spell, Ito Soda jammed a knife in his thigh to keep awake. When the vampire cat, disguised as O Toyo, entered the room of the sleeping prince, the soldier kept the feline away from the dying noble. The soldier was the first to realize that the cause of the prince's weakened state was the vampire cat. Everything else that had come into contact with the prince had been scrutinized, leaving only the vampire cat disguised in a woman's body, as the culprit.

The soldier followed the vampire cat, which was still disguised as O Toyo, back to its hiding place and tried to destroy it. The soldier failed, and the vampire returned to its original form as a feline and fled. When the prince regained his health, he organized a small army of men to head up to the mountains and eliminate the vampire.

Mismatched Lovers
Edward Lear's 1871 poem, "The Owl and the Pussy-cat," reveals in a comical manner the romantic experience of star-crossed lovers who move away and elope for everlasting happiness.

Please the Cat
The Quechua tribe of Peru feared a cat demon they called Ccoa. They believed the powerful, 3-foot feline controlled hail and lightning. To keep the cat happy, and hoping for protection of their crops and tribe members, they provided regular offerings.

Caped Crusader

The most powerful man of an ancient native tribe from Africa's Gold Coast was the leader, followed by the shaman. Their holy man would adorn his shoulders with cat skin to aid him in communicating with the spirit world.

FELINE PROVERBS THROUGHOUT THE AGES

Cats were among many animals used when proverbs began springing up in the days of oral storytelling. Some make sense, while others will have you shaking your head.

The cat knows whose lips she licks. −1023
The cat would eat fish but would not wet her feet. −1225
As the cat plays with a mouse −1340
When the cat's away, the mice will play. −1470
Beware of cats that lick from the front and claw from behind. −15th century
A cat has nine lives. −1546
All cats are gray in the dark. −1546
A cat in gloves catches no mice. −1573
Good liquor will make a cat speak. −1585
Never was a cat drowned that could see the shore. −1594
An old cat laps as much milk as a young one. −1605
A muzzled cat was never a good mouser. −1605
The scalded cat fears cold water. −1611
The cat has kittened in your mouth. −1618
As nimble as a blind cat in a barn −1639
Cats eat what hussies spare. −1683
To put a cat among pigeons −1706
He that plays with cats must expect to be scratched. −1710
He who hunts with cats will only catch rats. −1712
None but cats are allowed to quarrel in my house. −1732
Watch which way the cat jumps. −1825
Enough to make a cat laugh −1851
As busy as a cat in a tripe shop −1890

A CON-CAT-ENATION OF CAT FACTS

Top 10 Cat Names

Females:	**Males:**
Chloe	Tigger
Lucy	Max
Molly	Oliver
Sophie	Smokey
Zoe	Simon
Kitty	Charlie
Princess	Simba
Lily	Jack
Cleo	Tiger
Bella	Oscar

Channel Surfing
Twenty-two percent of cat owners say they watch TV programs they think their felines will enjoy.

It's All Greek to Me

The term "ailurophilia" refers to the love of cats, while "ailuro-phobia" is the fear of cats. *Ailurus* is the ancient Greek word for "cat," which was coined by Herodotus in the fifth century. The root word *ailuroi* means "tail waver."

 According to statistics, there are just as many male cats as there are females. Males outnumber females 65 to 35 in the feral world.

Not Really a Cat

The Man Who Loved Cat Dancing was a western movie produced in 1973 that starred Burt Reynolds, Sarah Miles, Lee J. Cobb, Jack Warden and George Hamilton. Cat is the name of a female character in the film.

Stay-at-Home Pets

Less than half of pet owners have taken their animals to work.

Feline Festivities

A survey found all respondents admitted to buying their cat a Christmas or Hanukkah present.

Eighty-seven percent of cat owners include their felines in holiday celebrations.

Let Me Entertain You

If you sing or dance for your cat, then you are part of the 65 percent of cat owners that entertain their pet in this manner.

At Your Beck and Call

More than half of cat owners say they have taken time off from work to nurse an ailing feline.

At least 50 percent of cat owners have made a special meal for their cat.

Twenty-two percent of cat owners say they watch TV programs they think their felines will enjoy.

Boys and Girls

A male cat is called a tom, and a female—of course—is a queen. A neutered male is called a gib.

Doe-cat is an old English term that was used for females.

Alternative names for male cats before the 18th century were boar-cat and ram-cat.

Counting Kittens
The average number of kittens born to a female is four to six.

Two's Company, Three's a...
A group of kittens or cats is called a clowder.

Straight Up

Cats are the only creatures that walk holding their tail vertically.

Female Fashion
Tortoiseshell, calico or patched tabby cats are almost always female because two X chromosomes are necessary to express the red gene to obtain those color patterns.

Fur of Arms

Lions and leopards were the felines of choice in heraldry because cats had a bad rep in the Middle Ages. But if you look hard and long, there are a few examples where kitty crept into position; in the Roman Temple of Liberty, a cat is seen at the feet of a goddess. "Touch Not the Cat Gloveless" is written under a cat on a Catanach bookplate.

Population Explosion

If left unchecked, the cat population could explode from the efforts of just one female. Using the model of a breeding pair that produces 14 offspring three times a year, in five years you'd have a cat coup. Presuming that all the kittens survived, that there were equal numbers of males and females and that breeding begins at age one, the possible number of kittens would be about 65,536, give or take a few.

Weighing In
The average weight of a cat of no particular pedigree is between 7 and 12 pounds.

Across or Down?

Cats show a preference for either vertical or horizontal scratching.

 Cats inhale 20 to 40 times per minute.

Against the Odds
The odds of a domesticated cat catching a mouse are one out of every three attempts.

Naming Names

In 1972, Claire Necker published a book called *Four Centuries of Cat Books* containing the names of 2293 books about cats.

Homeless Cats
Feral cats are a problem in several countries. To stem the rising tide of unwanted kitties, human measures have been implemented, such as licensing for pets and trap-and-release programs that capture homeless cats, then neuter or spay them and re-release them after surgery.

Buy This

Everyday we are bombarded with advertising, from newspapers to TV and billboards. And the minds behind the promotional campaigns have included cats in a variety of ways to promote products. Two of the most recognized cats featured prominently in advertising are the Black Cat on packages of Virginia cigarettes—also the name of the brand—and Morris, the finicky cat promoting cat food.

Two Americans collected and published three volumes of advertising material starring felines.

Cat Span

Since 1930, the life expectancy of household cats has doubled from 8 to 16 years. The lifespan of a stray cat is usually less than four years.

 The domestic cat does not appear in the Bible.

Fluid Displacement
When grooming, cats expend almost the same amount of water in saliva as they would discharge in urine.

> *One is never sure, watching two cats washing each other, whether it's affection, the taste or a trial run for the jugular.*
>
> –Helen Thomson

Super Savers
It is estimated that 10,000 animals were rescued following Hurricanes Rita and Katrina in the southern U.S. from the combined efforts of a variety of rescue organizations and volunteers. As a result of lessons learned from those natural disasters and the needs of pets, several states have passed laws to address concerns.

Pssst, Wanna Buy Some Nip?

A bit of weed, in this case catnip, provides about 80 percent of
the domestic cat population with an enjoyable yet somewhat
manic trip (the other 20 percent seem to have no interest in the
herb). A frenzy of rolling and flopping about on the floor for up
to 15 minutes is a typical response, followed by a request to head
down to the corner store for munchies. The perennial herb, when
inhaled or rolled in by cats, produces a euphoric reaction that has
been likened to a human's reaction to marijuana use.

Cat Scratch Clever

Cats have a remarkable weapon, a shovel and spurs disguised as
claws. Unlike other critters with fixed talons, felines keep their
daggers sheathed. Voluntary muscles engage the claws only
when needed, such as when they are trying to get your attention
by climbing your unprotected leg.

Pets of the Airwaves

A quick movement of the fingers on the computer can link cat owners online with the All Pets Radio Station. The Internet station features talk shows with hosts profiling all things pet related.

Anyone Can Be a Star

One of the most popular trends among many cat owners is to capture their felines on digital cameras and upload their antics onto YouTube. Creative filmmakers have their cats performing for millions of Internet viewers worldwide. Did I hear mews of Oscar?

Isn't it Nice to be Kneaded?

A cat rhythmically treading its front paws on your grandmother's handmade quilt isn't a sign of kitty's displeasure of her craftsmanship. The cat is demonstrating affection and trust by using a throwback behavior from kittenhood it used while nursing.

Rev That Purr

What does a diesel engine have in common with a cat?
The engine idles at 26 cycles per second, the same frequency as a purring cat.

All the Right Stuff

Landing on one's feet like a cat is more than just an expression. Born with a righting reflex, newborn kittens use it to compensate for their inability to walk or see.

If a cat is falling any kind of distance, a sequence of events occurs as a cat rights its body while plunging towards earth. As with an airborne freestyle boarder, finding the ground is the first step, so the head rotates. This leads to positioning the body horizontally and taking a spread-eagle approach prior to landing. While the tail acts like a rudder, the other muscles relax in anticipation of a four-point landing. This ability is not 100 percent foolproof, which is a good reason to ban cats from joining base-jumping clubs.

I'll Have a Pint of Milk, Please

Inns and pubs in Great Britain over several centuries have used "cat" in naming their establishments. A London tavern located in Long Lane in the early 1600s kept the name simple by just calling itself Cat. From 1810 to 1826, clerks of the Foreign Office would whet their whistles at the Cat and Bagpipe on the corner of Downing Street, Westminster.

One English saloon took a leap of faith dubbing their inn, Salutation and Cat. The significance behind the odd title goes back to when the angel Gabriel "greeted" Mary with news of the impending birth of Jesus. It is alleged that a cat was witness to the salutation.

One 1823 innkeeper in Eastcheap had a sense of humor, christening his tavern Cat and Kittens.

Today, having "cat" in the name of your club is just as trendy as it was 300 years ago. Some of Britain's newer haunts have stretched their imaginations to include the Cat and Cracker, Cat and Custard, Cat's Whiskers, Laughing Cat and Mad Cat.

On Your Mark, Get Set, Go

Cat racing during the 19th century in Belgium was a popular sport. The bizarre competition involved placing cats in cloth bags and at the stroke of midnight releasing them. The cat that reached home first was the winner and won a small prize for the owner. A blind cat won the last race ever held.

For a short time in England, cat racing was resurrected when a 220-yard track opened in Dorset in 1936. Felines were required to run after an electric mouse. A final kick at cat racing in 1949, near Kent, also failed to catch on.

 The placement of a cat's nose and eyes prohibit the feline from seeing those tidbits you placed under its nose.

The Better to See You With

Peripheral vision of a cat is roughly 285 degrees, and their long-range sight is about 120 feet.

Hearing in Surround Sound

Cat ears can rotate 180 degrees independently of one another, thanks to 32 muscles that control ear movement.

White Noise

Up to 85 percent of white cats with blue eyes, or with one blue eye and one different-colored eye, are deaf. A gene associated with the white coat color is the suspected culprit.

The smallest feline is a masterpiece.

–Leonardo da Vinci

Standing on End

When frightened, your cat might look like it got into a can of mousse as its hair stands straight out all over its body. But when it is in offense mode, the cat has a Mohawk hairstyle, with its fur standing up in a ridge along its spine.

CAT FACT

A newborn kitten typically weighs in at 3 to 4 ounces. Body length is roughly 5 inches. Within one week, a kitten will double in size.

Half Measures

Neutering males and spaying females is the most common operation performed on cats and has been conducted for more than a century. The reproductive organs of a male can be removed when the cat is six months old; for females, the process is usually done when the cat is four or five months old. Occasionally, some owners will request a procedure that keeps their cat's sexuality intact while preventing unwanted pregnancies. This surgery is also performed while the cat is under anesthesia—a female's fallopian tubes are tied, and a male's spermatic cord is snipped.

STAMP OF APPROVAL

Lick and Stick

Despite instant communication through email, some people still prefer to send a good, old-fashioned letter through the postal service. And to get that mail on its way, a stamp is required—you know where I am going with this. Countries around the world have issued a variety of stamps depicting domestic cats.

Catch Me if You Can

Argentina put out a sheetlet of stamps that included a cartoon depicting a smiling cat up in a tree with a dog at the foot of the trunk.

From the Land of Ice and Snow

Canada produced its first-ever cat stamp in 2004, a pair of cats in a common position—comfortably perched on an armchair.

Maltese Mew

It was a first for the tiny republic of Malta when they produced a set of stamps adorned with cats. In 2004, they issued a set of five stamps of feline head portraits.

Lotus Land Kitty

Japan has issued a gamut of cat stamps over the years, including paying homage to the country's most famous cat character, Hello Kitty. Taiwan, too, has issued Hello Kitty stamps.

A Stamp I Am

In March 2004, the United States honored Theodore Seuss Geisel, also known as Dr. Seuss, with a stamp that included his picture and the illustration of the Cat in the Hat.

Stamps that Taste like Lasagna

Cartoon cat Garfield was profiled twice, in different years, on Belgian stamps. The country also issued Disney stamps that included a kitten.

On Her Majesty's Service

Great Britain is no stranger to cat stamps. The Royal Mail issued 2006 postage that depicted a cat on one half and the word "Hello" on the other. Could it be a Hello Kitty knock-off?

Eine Kleine Kitty

A 2004 philatelic fair, or stamp festival, near Dusseldorf, Germany, unveiled a set of five cat stamps. Collectors were ecstatic to receive an out-of-the-ordinary cat cancellation mark—an indication that the stamp has been used—the same day. That's something philatelists (stamp collectors) get excited about.

Not Glue and Paper Again for Supper

Switzerland produced a cartoon stamp of Cocolino, a cat-chef character.

Hans Christian's Cat

Celebrating the bicentennial of Hans Christian Andersen's birthday in 2005, Singapore produced stamps depicting animal characters from his fairy tales, which also included a cat.

Custom Stamps

North Korea has shown its fondness for cats with several issues of cat stamps, including some featuring the traditional Asian native cat, the Siamese.

Dutch Treat

Though not quite as abundant as world-renowned Delft pottery produced in the Netherlands, many cat stamps have been issued by this tiny country throughout the years. A recent stamp features a cat beside a fisherman.

Cossack Cat

In a 2002 series of stamps depicting traditionally clad Ukrainians, the country managed to include a cat with one group. Another feline appeared in a sequel set three years later.

Cats for Kids

Malaysia chose to recognize Children's Day in 2003 with a stamp showing an attractive tabby cat.

One Good Lick Deserves Another

In 2006, a series of pet stamps issued by the Republic of China included an Abyssinian stamp and a stamp featuring a Norwegian forest cat.

Humor that Sticks

In the same year, France produced a set of stamps that featured Phillipe Getluck's cartoon creation *Le Chat*.

FELINE TREASURE TROVE

Cat Collectibles

Some people begin by owning a cat and then at some point become spellbound and begin amassing cat collectibles. Over the centuries since domestication, items in every medium have been produced immortalizing cats in every conceivable way. Ceramic, wood, glass, metal, paper, canvas and plastic cat objects fetch good money at live auctions and online. Some collectors are discerning about their collectable acquisitions, others may opt for a theme behind gathering cat treasures and some might just collect willy-nilly.

Let's Form a Club

The Cat Collectors' Club is an international organization that was initiated by American Marilyn Dipoye. It has more than 1000 members who receive a *Cat Collector's Catalog* and a bi-weekly newsletter called *Cat Talk*.

Hard Core Treasurer Hunters

Ceramics comprise the bulk of collector items. Kiln cats were produced from a variety of substance such as Chinese or English porcelain to clay figurines splashed with color. A 5.5-inch, blue and white, 17th-century tabby water container, possibly from Persia, has been valued at more than $2000. It was part of a collection donated to a museum.

Objects of Desire

Florence Groff of France didn't stop collecting cats with her four Siamese pets; she went on to break the record for the most amassed cat-related items. Groff began collecting feline memorabilia in

1979, and the last count was 11,717 articles. Among them are 2118 different cat figurines, 86 plates, 60 pieces of crystalware, 140 metallic boxes, 9 lamps, 36 stuffed toys, 41 painted eggs and 2666 cat postcards.

Heading

Mrs. Blanche Langton had an amazing collection of cat treasures. The Gloucester-born collector sourced her collection, which included pieces from before the birth of Christ, from Europe and Egypt. The pursuit of cat ornaments took Langton from flea markets to high-end stores. Before her death in 1974, she split the rare and exotic collection between the Norwich Museum, which received the cats created after 1 AD, and London University, which graciously took the cats that date to before the birth of Christ.

TOP 10 REASONS TO OWN A CAT

10. A daily dose of feline disdain keeps you humble.

9. Cat hair in your food adds protein.

8. You can throw out all your mousetraps.

7. Cheap entertainment. Cat…paper bag…need I say more?

6. Clean laundry and carpets are overrated.

5. A cat will happily chase down all creepy bugs that find their way into your home.

4. There is no such thing as "cat breath." Well, maybe "tuna breath"…

3. A hungry cat makes an excellent alarm clock.

2. Your cat is self-cleaning.

1. Happiness is a purring cat.

ABOUT THE AUTHOR

Diana Macleod

Diana MacLeod loves animals. She's the editor of two agricultural magazines, *Central Alberta Farmer* and *Western Dairy Farmer*. When she's not busy writing and editing, Diana can be found at home in the country with her family and two dogs, a horse, a donkey and as many as 20 cats. And if that's not enough, she helps out at her neighbor's dairy farm. In her spare time, Diana also enjoys motor sports, hockey, photography and travel.

ABOUT THE ILLUSTRATOR

Peter Tyler

Peter is a recent graduate of the Vancouver Film School visual art and design and classical animation programs. Although his ultimate passion is in filmmaking, he is also intent on developing his draftsmanship and storytelling, with the aim of using those skills in future filmic misadventures.

BLUE BIKE BOOKS

NOW ENJOY THESE FUN- AND FACT-FILLED BOOKS OF ONTARIO AND CANADIAN TRIVIA...

Bathroom Book of Ontario History

A comprehensive and entertaining collection of facts about Ontario's past. The province has been at the centre of many major events in North America since the earliest days of colonization, from the English-French Seven Years War, the exodus of United Empire Loyalists following the American Revolution, the War of 1812 with the U.S. and the very founding of Canada as a confederacy. This book recounts these and many other historic events in Ontario.

$9.95 • ISBN10: 1-897278-16-0 • ISBN13: 978-1-897278-16-1 • 5.25" X 8.25" • 168 pages

Weird Ontario Places

Canada's most populous province may also boast some of the weirdest places in the country. This enjoyable collection features hundreds of odd locales and structures, from a Cold War relic called the Diefenbunker to the world's largest curling stone to the home of the famous white squirrels.

$9.95 • ISBN10: 1-897278-07-1 • ISBN13: 978-1-897278-07-9 • 5.25" X 8.25" • 168 pages

Bathroom Book of Canadian Trivia

An entertaining and lighthearted collection of illustrated factoids from across the country. You'll find beasties—from the elusive lake monster Ogopogo to Canada's national emblem, the beaver—and you'll find culture and crime, such as the Calgary Stampede or the number of cars stolen in Canada and where they were stolen. This book has a myriad of informative tidbits to satisfy your curiosity and tickle your funny bone.

$9.95 • ISBN10: 0-9739116-0-3 • ISBN13: 978-0-9739116-0-2 • 5.25" X 8.25" • 144 pages

Bathroom Book of Canadian History

From wild weather to odd prime ministers, Canada's amazing history is full of the comic, the tragic and the just plain weird. You'll enjoy this fun collection of fascinating facts about our illustrious and often peculiar past.

$9.95 • ISBN10: 0-9739116-1-1 • ISBN13: 978-0-9739116-1-9 • 5.25" X 8.25" • 144 pages

Weird Canadian Places

The Canadian landscape is home to some pretty odd sights; for example, the UFO landing pad in St. Paul, Alberta, the ice hotel in Québec City or Casa Loma, Canada's only castle. This book humorously inventories many real estate oddities found across the country. Welcome to the True North—strange to see.

$9.95 • ISBN10: 0-9739116-1-1 • ISBN13: 978-0-9739116-1-9 • 5.25" X 8.25" • 168 pages

Available from your local bookseller or by contacting the distributor,
Lone Pine Publishing, at 1-800-661-9017.

www.lonepinepublishing.com